Cross Stitched

ONE MAN'S JOURNEY FROM RUIN TO RESTORATION

Two-time World Series Champion for the New York Yankees

JASON GRIMSLEY

with JASON CLARK

Fedd Books
P.O. Box 341973
Austin, TX 78734
www.thefeddagency.com

Published in association with The Fedd Agency, Inc., a literary agency.

Cover Design by Deryn Pieterse

ISBN: 978-1-957616-02-5

EISBN: 978-1-957616-03-2

Library of Congress Number: 2022905749

Printed in the United States of America

First Edition 22 23 24 25 26 – 3 2 1 12 11 10 9 8 7

Contents

Endorsements

"Cross Stitched is a powerful, indeed riveting, story. A story of triumph and pain, the highest of highs and the lowest of lows. It is a story of baseball, the love of a wife that won't give up, and the amazing grace of God."

Don't miss this book!

Pastor Jeff Wells. Woods Edge Church
in The Woodlands Texas

"Read this book and you will be blessed and encouraged!! It's an incredible story of Jesus and his redemptive power! it's an open and honest accounting of my friends life, and it has a very happy ending! I'm proud of Jason and Dana and consider them friends for life!"

Bo Mitchell, President-Game Day Memories and
Colorado Rockies Team Chaplain

"Jason is my former teammate, roommate, and now life-long friend. Over the years I have lost count of the number of times I have shared stories about my times with Grims, typically culminating in a chorus of laughter.

In Cross Stitched you will be introduced to a person I consider to be deeply loyal, fiercely loving, and intensely focused. You will also meet a man both strong and vulnerable enough to share stories in hopes that others benefit from his experiences.

I have met and known a lot of people around the game of baseball over the past thirty plus years, and none of them are quite as memorable as Grims. I am sure that you will feel the same after learning a bit more about his journey."

Jerry DiPoto, President, Baseball Operations,
Seattle Mariners

"I've walked with Jason for 20 years. I know the "tough guy" mask he wore and that it doesn't lead to a life truly lived. It leads to pain, emptiness and regret. Jason recognized there was an empty hole inside and only God could fill it. After realizing that "ending it" isn't the true competitor's mentality, by God's grace, Jason faced his battle, survived and chose to become the man God wanted him to be. The man he had been chasing all along. I'm so proud of Jason and his courage! His life is God breathed and his journey will help many others! Well done my friend! Well done Dana for standing strong and being an amazing teammate!"

Jeremy Affeldt, 3x World Series Champion,
Proud friend of Jason Grimsley

Acknowledgments

I want to start by thanking you, the reader, for your support. This book is a forthright and often blunt glimpse into the craziness that was and still is my life. I consider myself the luckiest man on the face of the earth (plagiarism at its finest). Not because of what I did, but because of what God has allowed. Through the bad times and the good times, He was always there, and His plan was always exactly what I needed. It's taken a long time to see it, but over the years, and by His grace, the scales are being removed and my eyes and heart opened.

The people I need to thank are countless. I'm sure I will miss a few, but just know I'm eternally grateful to you all. This is your story as well as mine. Life is not lived through a single set of eyes but through a community of others that helps to shape and mold everyone they touch.

My family. Dana, you are the love of my life. You stood by me when I was at my worst. You gave me love when I couldn't love myself. You believed in me when I was hopeless. And you forgave me when I felt as if I was unforgivable. You exemplify the love of Christ. You are my best friend, my solid foundation, my voice of reason and you will always be my sunshine. I love you.

Hunter, John, and Rayne. You are my pride and joy. I'm so grateful God blessed me with three amazing children. I'm so proud of each of you. When I look at the way you all have grown into confident, loving, and caring young adults, I truly see the miracle in God's design.

It is a testament to each of your willingness to love when life became hard. That is an amazing attribute I know you will carry for the rest of your lives. The love you have for the Lord is apparent in the way each of you live your lives. For that, I consider myself a blessed man. You are the greatest gift God has bestowed upon me on this earth. I love you more than you know.

Mom and Dad. You guys are my heroes. Without your love and guidance, I would never have made it. Dad, you taught me the value of work. You showed me that anything is possible if you just get it done. No excuses, no doubt, just give it your best. You taught me how to learn under any circumstance and that success is getting up just one more time. You taught me how to be confident. You taught me how to be a man.

Mom, you gave me the ability to love fiercely. You were the soft art to Dad's hard art. You gave me compassion and kindness. You have always been there to listen to me. You were the quiet voice that could always calm me down. You are still the one I call every day. I love our talks and always have. When I was alone at such a young age, I knew you were always there. That helped me more than you can imagine. Words cannot describe the love I have for you two. Thank you for being my parents. Thank you for the love, support, and belief in me and my family.

Little Brother. You made growing up worthwhile. Despite our knockdown drag-outs when we were young, I always knew you had my back. I will always cherish our time spent together. The hunting, fishing, biking, baseball games in Mamaw's front yard, the football games, the motorcycle rides down the fire lanes—all of it was with you. Thank you for keeping me out of more trouble than I got into. Thank you for not always telling on me. Yes, Mom and Dad, I got away with more than I didn't. I love you, brother.

Lynn, I love you like the sister I never had. Thank you for the love you have for me and my family. It can be a bit crazy at times, but you handle it with grace and understanding. Thank you for loving Joe like you do.

Sean. How did we make it this far? That we have is truly a miracle. Buddy, I want to thank you and your family for helping to raise me. Linda and Jay were like my second set of parents. And you were my other brother growing up. The memories we made will always hold a special place in my heart. Running from the game warden, chasing after the law (Van, you know who), and many other stories we can't tell. I love you, Wanda, and your family. Thank you for always being there.

Terry. My brother from another mother. I cannot thank you enough for all that you have done for me and my family. I still think our parents were up to something! We are so much alike. Kindred spirits, so to speak. I know I can tell you anything and you will always give me an answer. I might not like it, but you will tell me the truth. The fact I have a man I can be venerable with is more special to me than you can imagine. You know my secrets. You know my fears. You know my heart. You know me and I am thankful you love me. Love you, buddy.

Pam, thank you for loving us the way you do. It brings my heart joy to see Terry happy like he is. You are such a blessing to us all. We love you more than you know.

Coach Lynch and Nancy, I miss you. I love you. I didn't get to say that enough. You will always be my coach. Others were men who taught me how to play a game. You were the man who taught me how to love the game and life. You treated me like a son. You let me live life with you and made sure I was taking advantage of the opportunity you created for me. You are the reason I played the game for twenty-two years. You were the reason I succeeded. You built the foundation that held me steady through any situation I faced. I am eternally grateful. I would love to have a catch again someday. OMAHA!

Nancy, thank you so much for putting up with a crazy young man. Thank you for loving me like you do. I will always cherish the time spent with you and Rick. Those were some of the best days of my life. You were always a calm voice during the madness. I loved every minute with you guys. I will always be just a call away. Thank you for sharing Rick with me. Love you and your family so much.

My in-laws. Barbara, Reid, Stan, Phyllis, Tom, Ginger. I want to thank you for your love and support. You guys did an amazing job raising a wonderful woman I have the privilege to call my wife. It's not hard to see why she is the person she is. All the siblings, Tommy, Diane, Brad, Victoria, Wendy and Chess, you have a special place in my heart. There is no way we would be where we are today without you and your love. I do not look at any of you as my in-laws. I see you as moms and dads, brothers and sisters. I'm so thankful to God for the gift you are to me and my family. You have always been there, and I will always love each of you for that.

God. Lord, I am humbled by the fact that you love me despite all of my daily shortcomings. You gave me life and then you gave me Life. I have no idea what is ahead, but I know it will be perfect. Thank you for the blessing that was yesterday. Thank you for the blessing of today. And if tomorrow should not come with me in it, thank you for loving me enough to send your only Son Jesus to die for my sins so that I may live for eternity in your presence. I love you, Lord.

CHAPTER ONE

Footprints

A VERY GOOD DAY

I was a new member of the New York Yankees: the team seven billion people identify with baseball, America's favorite pastime, and the team of legends like Babe Ruth, Lou Gehrig, Mickey Mantle, Yogi Bera, Whitey Ford, and Joe DiMaggio.

April 25, 1999, was Joe DiMaggio Day at Yankee Stadium—and the day I was baptized by George McGovern, the team chaplain. A few weeks earlier, I'd accepted Jesus as my Lord and Savior, and I couldn't imagine a better way to start my new season than with God and the Yankees.

It was a very good day.

The baptism took place at Lake Armonk, New York, just north of the city. The lake was beautiful and calm; it reflected the trees near its banks, the browns and greens merging in the early morning sun. My beautiful, pregnant wife Dana and my sons, Hunter and John, were there. A few of my new teammates came, too—Scott Brosius, Andy Pettitte, and Chad Curtis—guys who were excited about the new-found faith of a ruffian like Jason Grimsley.

George began by asking me if I accepted Jesus as my personal Savior. I gave a heartfelt yes and he put me under the water. Being dunked was a wonderful feeling marking a moment, a yes given to God, life, love, and forgiveness. I kept my eyes open the whole time. I wanted to see and experience everything. The water was cold for this East Texas boy, and yet I remember feeling a warmth. I came out of the water filled with joy and thankfulness. Still dripping wet and smiling the whole time, I hugged George, then Dana, the kids, and my teammates.

It was a very good day.

From there we all headed to Yankee Stadium for a Sunday game against the Toronto Blue Jays. When I walked into the clubhouse, it was full of Yankee Hall of Famers like Yogi Berra and Whitey Ford. And there was Ron Guidry, Goose, Catfish Hunter—the greats, heroes who'd won World Series with the Yanks. As I walked around shaking hands, I felt like a ten-year-old in a candy store.

Eventually I made my way to my locker. Our centerfielder, Bernie Williams, whose locker was next to mine, was sitting there, playing his guitar—and Bernie can play. He'd offered to give me a few pointers, so I'd left my guitar in my locker. Except it wasn't in my locker. Somebody was sitting in my chair playing my guitar! "Who the hell is sitting in my chair playing my guitar?" I thought. It was Paul Simon. Paul Simon was playing my guitar!

"And here's to you, Mrs. Robinson,

Jesus loves you more than you will know, wo wo wo…

Where have you gone, Joe DiMaggio?…"[1]

Of course Paul Simon was there on Joe DiMaggio Day. Later, he played for the fans, but in that moment, he played for just a handful of ballplayers. I sat in awe and listened to Bernie and Paul jam until I was distracted by Billy Crystal. If you know anything about William Edward Crystal, it's that he is uncomfortable when his date makes intimate noises in a restaurant and that he loves the Yankees—and not in that order. Billy Crystal was a clubhouse regular, but this was all new to me. He was wearing the blue pinstripes, and he wanted to play catch.

"I'll play catch with you," I said. So, we went out to the field to throw. I didn't give him any heat, but he could catch and throw. He's a surprisingly good athlete. He is also friendly and hilarious. The way he interacted with the fans and with me was perfect. I don't know how long we played catch, but I remember laughing the whole time.

It was a very good day.

We had a one run lead on the Blue Jays in the ninth inning. Then Mariano Rivera went out on the field. He's hands down the best closer that's ever played, probably the best that will ever play. If you want to get out of a game with a win, he's the pitcher you put in. With Mariano in, the game was as good as won. Except, Mariano gave up a run. I think it was the only save he blew all year. That's when I got the call. I took the mound in Yankee Stadium at capacity. 49,642 rowdy fans—my family among them—watched as I threw two scoreless and we won in the eleventh inning. This was my first win as a pitcher for the New York Yankees.

It was a very good day.

The clubhouse gave us a reservation at Smith and Wollensky, the steakhouse that ends all arguments. The manager, a great guy I know to this day, had a table set up with a bottle of wine and a note that read, "Congratulations on your first win!" Walking in there with Dana and the boys, I was full to bursting.

A quick recap: on April 25th, 1999, I was baptized by George McGovern, experienced the love of Jesus with my family and friends, played guitar with Paul Simon and catch with Billy Crystal, got my first win as a Yankee on Joe DiMaggio Day, and celebrated with my family at Smith and Wollensky.

It was a very good day.

I love telling this story because it got most of the good parts of my life in a moment. It marked a day when God and family and dreams and a sense of wholeness converged; where heaven marked my experience. It was a day when I felt whole, alive, and fulfilled. A day when God was with me. And I *knew* God was with me. But for every day I've known God was with me, I've had a hundred days when I've wondered where He was. And those days are some of the darkest.

A VERY BAD DAY

August 21, 2015

I was desperate and alone at my cousin's cabin in the woods. I'd consumed close to an ounce of cocaine and no telling how many bottles of vodka. It wasn't enough. After three days of failing to snort and drink myself to death, I made a decision. I sat down and wrote a note to everyone I loved. I told Dana she deserved better and how sorry I was for ruining her life. I apologized to my children for being a bad father. I let my mom and dad know it was not their fault. I said good-bye to my brother and thanked him for all the good memories. I let everyone know they mattered to me. Then I snorted the last bit of cocaine, drank another glass of vodka, picked up my pistol, and walked into the woods.

It was hot. Mid-August in East Texas hot. I walked through briars, thickets, ditches, around and over fallen trees. I walked until I didn't. Then I sat down, cocked the gun, put the barrel to my left eye, and pulled the trigger.

I SHOULD BE DEAD

I should be dead; I should've died more times than I can count.

When I was one, I bit into an electrical cord, I could have fallen forward against the wall of our 1940s rental house. Instead, I fell backward. Mom happened to see, realized what was happening, and jerked the live wire (and death) out of my mouth.

When I was five, Dad put me on his horse, Doc. Dad roped and saddled broncs when he was young until he got thrown against a fence. It was calves after that. Something spooked the thousand-pound animal and that horse took off, slipped, went down, and rolled completely over me. Dad came running, thinking I was dead. But I stood up, no worse for wear—just a muddied, confused boy proud to have amazed my dad by surviving.

When I was ten, I fell twenty feet from my hunting stand, landed flat on my back and just winded myself.

At eighteen, I blew my three-wheeler's engine going 50 mph on Highway 105, and it seized the back tires. I rode that front wheel to a stop like my life depended on it. It probably did.

In my twenties, I hit a curve at 120 mph while driving my brother's Suzuki Katana 750. I had to make a split-second decision: the ditch or the telephone pole. I chose the ditch, but damn, it was close.

On Lake Livingston by the dam, I wiped out going 50 mph, got knocked unconscious by my water ski, and went limp face down in the water. My friend Mark—a big old boy, thank God—jerked my limp body into the boat.

Then there was the time a twin-engine airplane crashed into my living room; five people died. Had I not stopped at the dealership on the way home to check a noise in my truck, it could've been seven dead, 'cause I'd have been sitting on the sofa in that room with my five-year-old daughter.

I should be dead a hundred times over, whether because of high-speed wrecks, more ditches than you've got time for, nearly drowning, or being crushed or electrocuted. Or that time my dad shot me in

Louisiana. Or that time my brother shot me in Mexico. Then there was that very bad day when I was 47 and I pulled the trigger.

When I try counting my near-deaths, I'm baffled I'm still here. And thankful for God's direction. I am still learning about miracles and how God's sovereignty works. I understand now that the pistol didn't go off because of a safety feature; a pressure plate that the palm of your hand compresses for the hammer to fall. I understand that I'm still breathing today because when I turned the pistol around, I failed to engage the pressure plate.

But breathing isn't always living. I can promise you that.

To me, the miracle isn't that the gun didn't fire, it's that I didn't try again. And the miracle is my journey since, the steady reconciling love I have experienced from God, family, and friends.

As to the sovereignty of God, I'm no great theologian, but I don't think it has much to do with what Jason Grimsley has or hasn't done in his life. I think it has everything to do with what Jesus did at the cross. And not just what Jesus did, but what He revealed about God's love for us.

FOOTPRINTS

"My God, my God, why have you forsaken me?"[2] That's what Jesus cried out on the cross on His darkest day—the worst imaginable bad day. I think that cry captures the worst pain we could know. It's a cry of confusion and sorrow and loss and so much disappointment.

I've cried out these same words in my own life: "My God, my God, why have you forsaken me?" Except, when I've cried out, I was pretty certain I knew why God would leave me. I'd screwed up. Again. I was unworthy and deserved to be left. I'd earned whatever I got. At least, that's what I thought.

But I have discovered two things. First, I don't get a say in how

God feels about me; Jesus already determined my worth at the cross, and He thought I was worth dying for. Second, God never leaves.

Yeah, for every day I've known God was with me, I've had a hundred days when I've wondered where He was. But that's changing. I'm learning and becoming convinced of this one thing: God has never left me. God does not leave.

I don't remember where I first saw the picture, but during the 80s it pretty much hung in every church entry, retirement center lobby, YMCA, rec center, and above the toilet at every grandma's house across America. Most people my age have read it, likely when they were discouraged, at the rec center for an AA meeting, or when peeing at their friend's grandma's house. It's an image of a beach at dusk. Just past where the water breaks upon the sand is one set of footprints. Next to those footprints is a poem.

> One night I dreamed a dream.
> As I was walking along the beach with my Lord,
> across the dark sky flashed scenes from my life.
> For each scene, I noticed two sets
> of footprints in the sand,
> one belonging to me
> and one to my Lord.
> When the last scene of my life shot before me
> I looked back at the footprints in the sand.
> There was only one set of footprints.
> I realized this was at the lowest
> and saddest times of my life.
> This always bothered me
> and I questioned the Lord
> about my dilemma.

"Lord, You told me when I decided to follow You,
You would walk and talk with me all the way.
But I'm aware that during the most troublesome
times of my life, there is only one set of footprints.
I don't understand why, when I needed You most,
You leave me."
He whispered, "My precious child,
I love you and will never leave you,
never, ever, during your trials and testings.
when you saw only one set of footprints
it was then that I carried you."[3]

I've loved that poem my whole life, and I love it more now. Every time I read it, I get a little choked up because I feel like I've lived it. In some of my toughest times, I've asked, "Why did you leave me?" Or, like Jesus cried out, I've wondered why God had forsaken me. But when I look back, I know without a doubt God never left me. In fact, He did just the opposite.

Did you know that moment on the cross, when Jesus cried out in the same desperation that I have felt, He was quoting the first verse of Psalm 22? David—a poet king who had some very bad days, days where he wondered where God was—wrote Psalm 22. While David couldn't have realized it when he wrote this psalm, the imagery he used to describe his pain was a prophetic picture of what Jesus literally experienced on the cross many years later.

In that Psalm David wrote phrases like:

"I am poured out like water, and all my bones are
out of joint."

"My mouth is dried up like a potsherd, and my
tongue sticks to the roof of my mouth."

"Dogs surround me, a pack of villains encircles me;
they pierce my hands and my feet. All my bones are
on display; people stare and gloat over me. They
divide my clothes among them and cast lots for my
garment."[4]

It's amazing how David's Psalm foretold what Jesus would experience. But to me, the most amazing thing about Psalm 22 is verse
24: "For he (God) has not despised or scorned the suffering of the
afflicted one; he has not hidden his face from him but has listened to
his cry for help" (emphasis mine).

So, Jesus was on a cross, experiencing the worst day in human
history, suffering beyond what I have suffered, crushed by sorrow,
disappointment, and the horrors of sin. He felt what every person on
this planet has felt during the saddest and most troublesome time of
His life: "There was only one set of footprints."

And then Jesus quoted from a Scripture passage that reveals that
during trials and testing, when we see only one set of footprints, it
is then that our Father carries us. Even when I have felt God was far
away, that I couldn't be more separated from Him, I have come to
believe God was with me. I have come to believe those were the times
He carried me.

I think the power of the gospel, or good news of salvation, is simply this: God is love and He never leaves. This is good news worth
writing about.

MY STORY

This book is not my attempt to preach, and I didn't write it to try to convert you in some way. I simply want to tell my story in hopes that it might resonate and encourage you in your story. And it is a wild one full of near-death experiences and epic days of life and love. It's full of fights and friendships, my brushes with fame and the law, faithfulness and betrayal, family and forgiveness, hope and loss, and baseball—from little league to the World Series. And of days when all was lost but for God.

I want to share about the very good days of love, my wide open, hundred-mile-an-hour approach to everything. My barefoot and rowdy childhood days riding bikes and hunting with my brother, the naive ambition and untamed hopes of my youth, the fun of fighting, conquering, comradery, and teamwork. I want to share about friendship and faithfulness, my all-out assault on a baseball career and the day I went pro, the love of my life, the world-changing wonder of fatherhood, the joy of Mom and Dad's pride—and the wonder that is life.

I also want to share about the very bad days. The deep unexplainable fear of being alone that I occasionally felt as a child. The shame I walked with for most of my life from being molested by the neighbor kid and becoming the quietly angry young man who wouldn't ever be taken advantage of again. The neurosis of hiding my shame until I snapped and nearly killed a man; the fights that were necessary and the fighting to hide my fears. The growing burden of condemnation, the pain I caused those I loved, and the painful end of my baseball career when I briefly became the face for an FBI witch hunt into performance-enhancement drugs. And finally, the dark days of disappointment, drugs, drink, infidelity, loss, and desperation.

I want to tell you the whole story so I can tell you about forgiveness, mercy, and grace; about my wife and the power of her love; of family and faithfulness and becoming vulnerable with a God who redeems, reconciles, and restores—a God who does not leave.

You see, I've been the hustler and the hustled, the bullied and the bully. I learned to survive by striking first, to defend by attacking, to win, to prove before anyone can disprove. I've earned my way in an unrelenting world—made it to the top and broke my body, heart, and spirit on the cruel systems of ego and striving. And I've been to the bottom, to hell, and I've learned like David wrote in another of his psalms: "If I ascend into heaven, You are there; If I make my bed in hell, behold, You are there."[5] I've learned that God doesn't leave; He is with me, He carries me.

I've known the praise of man, the success and excess of winning in a world defined by the winners. And God was with me.

I've been a self-made man, my own savior. I've died on the cross of my ego. And God was with me.

I've been the prodigal son and the older brother. Hell, I've been both on the same day! I've been lost and found and lost and found again. And God was with me.

I've discovered life and life more abundantly. And death? I know about that, too. I've tasted heaven and made my bed in hell. Even there, God was with me.

I've known a mercy that can't be earned. I have discovered that I am forgiven; nothing I do separates me from God's kindness. And I've tasted grace—a heart-, mind-, and soul-transforming grace. I've met the girl, captured her heart, and broken her heart. I've learned that love is a feeling and more than a feeling; it's a revelation that doesn't come until it's given away. I've discovered you can't give away what you don't have. That's worth noting. I've become better at recognizing the love I've received. As John wrote, "We love because God loved first loved."[6]

I've discovered what it is to be a dad, and to be a son; how to fail and succeed and say I'm sorry. And not just to say it, but to let it change you. That's a big lesson—and it's one I'm still learning.

I have a through line for this book, a thought that holds the whole thing together. You'll notice it in every chapter, whether I'm high or low, in heaven or hell: "nothing can ever separate us from God's love. Neither death nor life, neither angels nor demons, neither our fears for today nor our worries about tomorrow—not even the powers of hell can separate us from God's love."[7] God has never left me. He doesn't leave. And on the very bad days, though I may not feel it at the time, I can look back and know those were the days when He carried me. He was there when I went under the water with my family and friends close by. He was there when I was throwing ball with Billy Crystal in Yankee Stadium and when I was throwing my first win. He was there when I was stumbling in blind desperation through the woods with a pistol in my hand. He was there before I pulled the trigger, and after.

By faith I am learning that the one set of footprints is simply the evidence that He carried me, that God is love and He never leaves. And this is changing everything.

There is nothing more valuable to me, more life changing and transformational, more important than this one thing: I am loved by My God, and His love never fails.

So, this is my story to date. I'm only fifty-four, so it's not done being written yet. It's a story of incredible highs and incredible lows, but ultimately, it's a story about the reconciling love of God.

REVELATION

Revelation is when we simply see what was always there. It's when we discover what has always been true. It's when the hidden is made plain. And revelation is always followed by a sense of righteousness, peace, and joy—markers of the kingdom of God as Paul noted in Romans 14:17: "For the kingdom of God is not a matter of eating and drinking, but of righteousness, peace, and joy in the Holy Spirit."

Revelation is about transformation because the truth sets us free.

I think revelation is the whole point to this journey; to discover that God is good and His love endures forever and then realize it's truer than I ever imagined.

Throughout this book I will note those revelation moments in my life, when I saw what was good, what was always true, and how it changed me—even when I didn't know God was walking with me. I will note the moments that were extraordinary, the epiphanies that transformed everything, and the days when the clouds parted, and I saw clearly.

Revelation means to see God and His creation reconciled. It's the veil torn between us and God so we might experience salvation, resurrection, a life of living loved—the truth that sets us free.

CHAPTER TWO

The Whole Story

FAMILY IS THE LONG GAME

To me, family is everything; it's the whole story, and I am simply part of it. When it comes to family, I grew up with a good one. That's not to say we we're perfect—far from it. We had our messes, missteps, broken experiences, and skeletons exorcised from closets. But surrounding it all—the good, bad, and ugly—was and is love. The same reconciling love of God that never leaves or forsakes me.

My family and I loved each other fiercely, warts and all. Still do. And when love is the foundation, family is beautiful—even when it's sometimes broken or heartbreaking. If love is the beginning and end, family is also a generational, transformational journey.

I grew up loved and surrounded by family. I never had any doubt that they had my back the best way they knew how—and I've had theirs in the same way. We loved each other even on the days when love was delivered through the filters of past dysfunction or in the limitations of understanding. And this—knowing we have limitations to our understanding—is a big deal. Yeah, grace is available for our thoughts, too.

I think family is a loaded word for most of us; it's messy and sometimes broken. But the more I discover the never-leaving love of God, the more I'm convinced family is the whole story. And by that,

I mean family is the story God is telling. Or, as my friend Jason Clark says, "Family is the long game." It is the timeless story Jesus walked the planet to reveal and invite us into.

Jesus called God "Dad," and He called us brothers and sisters. He entered a family; He had a mom and dad, siblings, friends. He had a past, present, and future. He went through infancy and boyhood. He experienced messes, sometimes broken and sometimes heartbreaking. He stepped into a generational, transformational journey. I love that, especially as I dive into my childhood with you.

The fact that Jesus discovered and grew sure in His heavenly Father's love while growing up in the same messes and brokenness of earth is beyond encouraging—it's an invitation into all that is possible. You see, while I didn't know my heavenly Father like Jesus knew His growing up, my heavenly Father was still walking through my childhood with me. In hindsight, I can see how my family story—past, present, and future—fit within the grand family story God is telling. I think family is ultimately the story God is telling. And when I look at my family, I see the long game, the whole story; and I am amazed by the unfailing love of God in my family, even when we didn't know it.

TARKINGTON PRAIRIE

If I'm in a hurry, I tell people I'm from Cleveland, Texas, a town just north of Houston. Most folks can find it on a map. But I actually grew up in Tarkington Prairie, which sits east of Cleveland and is just three red lights and a Jack in the Box. Blink, and you'll miss it.

Just before you get into town, you'll pass a church next to a Sonic. The church is where the grocery store used to be, and that's where we hung out after class in high school.

Most people think *Fight Club* was a fictional secret group from a Brad Pitt movie by the same name, but anyone who grew up in the

70s in Tarkington Prairie, Texas, knows Fight Club was just what happened every day after school in the grocery store parking lot next to the Sonic. The girls would gossip and the boys, well, we'd sling fists.

Everybody knew everybody in Tarkington, and everybody knew everybody in that parking lot. So, it wasn't mean spirited, and we weren't trying to maim—it was just boys being boys, thinking the girls were impressed. Sometimes they were.

"You ready? Let's go!" someone would yell. Then we'd throw blows. If you knocked a guy down, you picked him up. After it was all done, we'd say, "Alright, I'll see you guys tomorrow."

Around the corner, and there weren't many corners in my hometown, there was a single-screen theater. I'd go to the movies once in a blue moon; first with my younger brother Joe and my mom, later with Joe and my buddies or a girl. The first movie I remember seeing there was *Smokey and the Bandit*. I loved that law-breaking, fast-driving, troublemaking Texan.

The hospital I was born in is still there but sits empty. Babies are born and stitches given in Cleveland now. I spent a lot of time there as a kid, though—and only one of those times (my birth) wasn't for an emergency or injury.

Tarkington is small, but there's no town small enough in Texas as to only have one church. My Mammaw's church was just down the road from Nanny's. Nanny was Dad's mom. She was Methodist. She was a good woman who did her best to provide a home for my dad. My dad hardly knew his father, and the little he did know was not kind.

My mom grew up Mormon. We called my mom's mom Mammaw. She was a Christ-follower and the sweetest lady God ever put on this earth. I never heard her raise her voice. She never had anything bad to say about anybody. The worst thing she could ever be accused of is occasionally, if traffic was bad, she'd say, "I wonder where everybody's going." That was Mammaw's version of road rage. She was just an incredible lady.

Mammaw's husband, my Papaw—well, where Mammaw was gentle and patient, Papaw was rough around the edges. Patience wasn't a virtue he was friendly with unless he was with Mammaw or in church. But Papaw and pretty much everyone else in my family left the churchgoing to Mammaw. She went every Sunday, and I attended only when Mom thought we should. I grew up never doubting God was real and our family had a sense of respect for His laws and the Good Book, but I never gave Him much thought or did much reading of the Bible. Except, of course, on the rare occasions I sat in Mammaw's church.

And that one time I visited a friend's Baptist church just up the road.

I was ten, and it was a Wednesday night revival meeting or something like that. I sat with my buddies and listened to the preacher pontificate. Something must have landed when the altar call was given, because I got up and I went down front. It was sincere, and for a minute I felt called. But it wasn't revelation. No hidden things were made plain, it was just a brief crossing of paths; a brief moment when I realized God might be walking with me.

But Tarkington was too full of wild adventures for a wildling like me to spend time wondering about God's footprints. I had squirrels to hunt, alligators to trap, fish to catch, bicycles to ride, motorbikes to jump, fires to start, ballgames to play, cigarettes to secretly smoke, tree forts to build, fists to sling. There were battles to be won, land to be taken, and every other amazing boyhood adventure Tarkington Prairie could offer.

We lived out in the country, and by we, I mean Dad, Mom, my

younger brother Joe, and me, as well as my grandparents, uncles, and aunts. We were surrounded by cow fields and trees, thousands of acres owned by the timber company, so there was plenty for Joe and me to discover and conquer.

Joe was my best friend. Until I left Tarkington after high school, we pretty much did everything together. I'm older by two years, which meant I led the way on most of our adventures. It also meant I took the lion's share of any whoopings we experienced because of them. We fought like cats and dogs but always had each other's backs.

We were raised in the 70s with no video games, iPhones, or computers. We were too busy for TV, and everything we did was outside regardless of the season. In the 70s we also didn't have helmets, seatbelts, knee pads, or elbow pads; I don't think they'd been invented yet.

We left the house in the morning and played until it was dark, or until Mom whistled for us to come home for dinner. We wore jeans in the winter and cut off jean shorts in the summer, 'cause that's what boys from east Texas wore in the 70s. Hell, that's still what they wear. Shirts were optional, of course, and we were barefoot most of the time.

Outside of school, we spent our days riding our bicycles down fire lanes that the logging company had cut through the landscape. They crisscrossed the land with one running right by our house. We could go anywhere on them, and we did: lakes, ponds, rivers, land that was perfect for hunting and fishing. We'd even ride our bikes all the way into Cleveland so we could go to Wal-Mart. It was an old-school strip mall original back then. On good days, when we had scrounged up a few nickels, we might buy a hot dog fried in cornmeal, because there's nothing better than a corn dog. But we could never stay long, though, because Mom would've killed us if she knew we'd biked so far away. She would've asked, "What were you thinking?" And that question probably would've been followed by Dad's belt.

WHAT WERE YOU THINKING?

Maybe the best way to describe myself is to tell you how my mom describes my little brother, Joe: "Now Joe, he would think about stuff before he'd do it."

"What were you thinking?" is a phrase I've heard my whole life. I can't remember the first time it was said to me, but that's likely because I was still too young to comprehend the English language. Mostly, this question came just before getting my ass whooped by Dad.

Like that time when I melted his brand-new cooler because it was the perfect size to support the ramp I built so I could jump my bike over the fire. Or like that time I shot Joe in the face with my new BB Gun. Dad got them for us and nodded in agreement with Mom's stern warning, "Don't shoot each other!" But when six-year-old Joe came around the corner I was hiding behind, the BB hit and stuck about an inch below his right eye. He cried as I dug it out while begging him, "Don't tell Mom!" He told Mom.

"What were you thinking?" Mom asked. I got my ass whooped when Dad got home. I think this question was a generous way for them to wonder about my hundred-mile-per-hour-at-a-brick-wall personality. But when the question was asked with a temper, it changed to, "What's wrong with you?" And I've heard that question my whole life, too. Hell, I might have heard it just yesterday.

"What's wrong with you?" is a lot like "What were you thinking?" except it's more of a statement than a question. Admittedly, there just may be something wrong with me.

You see, "Can I get hurt doing this?" isn't a thought I've ever had—not once. It has never crossed my mind while accelerating, during a climb, or before throwing a fist. That said, I can't tell you how many times the thought, "This is gonna hurt," has flashed through my mind in the split second before the crash, fall, or fist to the jaw.

I have always been 100 miles an hour or parked in the garage.

I have always been 120 watts or lights out.

I have two settings, go or asleep.

There's no halfway in me, I am all in or all out; no lukewarm, just hot or cold.

As a kid I was a daredevil and always pushing the limits, which meant lots of exciting edge-of-my-seat moments and lots of pain. Thankfully, I've always had a high pain tolerance and a quick recovery time. And it's a good thing, because I have a list of injuries a mile long. If hospitals gave out punch cards where the tenth visit was free, I'd have been good for a free visit or two. One of the nurses that worked the emergency room once told Mom, "Judy, if I didn't know you, I'd turn you in to Child Protective Services." I was in there for everything from cuts on my face, legs and hands, to broken wrists and arms, and then there was that time I lost an appendage.

FROM KX 80 TO ER

I remember the day Dad came home with KX 80 motorbikes. I was twelve and Joe was ten. And they were awesome. Dad went to Conroe, Texas, to buy them and didn't tell Mom why he went. She wasn't too happy with Dad that day. More than a hundred times since, Mom has said, "I had a sinking feeling in my stomach when he brought those motorcycles back."

Her "sinking feeling" was for good reason. One week to the day Dad brought those bikes home, I lost my left big toe and part of my foot. I was riding between my grandmother's and my aunt's houses, as fast as I could make that bike go at 45 miles an hour. The grass was about a foot and a half high—and just tall enough to hide the foot-tall tree stump. My foot was hanging down, and I hit the stump at full speed.

Thank God for Mom's, and therefore Dad's, mandatory helmet rule. I remember flying off the bike with, "This is gonna hurt," flashing through my mind. I hit the ground in a violent headlong tumble that ended with me flat on my back. I sat up and took account: my neck worked, my arms were good, and my hands seemed fine, but my foot was bleeding. There was blood gushing from between the big toe and the next toe.

"I'm gonna need stitches," I thought as I reached down to investigate. I picked my foot up and my toe fell over as if it wasn't attached to the rest of my foot. Except, it was. A tendon was the only thing holding it on. I remember seeing all the ligaments and blood vessels, blue and white. I squeezed it back together. And I think that's when I went into shock. I was sort of rocking when my brother drove up to me, saw the blood and my state, and raced to get Mom.

Meanwhile, my Papaw had heard the crash. He came out but was completely out of commission by the time he reached me. He had emphysema so bad he couldn't do anything more than try and catch his breath, which was what he was still doing when Mom arrived. She had run from the house and panicked when she saw my foot. She fell to the ground and started beating it crying out, "I don't know what to do!" over and over. If I hadn't already been in shock, that would've done it.

My grandfather finally had enough breath to say, "Judy!" That snapped Mom out of it. "I'll get the car!"

Mom nodded, stood up, and then pulled one of those superhero moves—the kind of story you read about in *Reader's Digest* (or if you're under thirty, online). You know, the story where mom lifts the car off her kid. Except my superhero 5'2", 105-pound mom lifted her 90-pound twelve-year-old son and carried him like a baby about forty-five yards to the car.

I never let go of my foot. I squeezed it while she carried me, while she wrapped a towel around it, and while she drove like a maniac to the emergency room. "Mom, slow down! You're gonna kill us both before we get there!" I yelled as I was tossed around in the back seat.

I didn't feel the pain until they put me on a gurney. And then I felt more pain than the devil on resurrection Sunday. It felt like someone was putting a blowtorch to my foot. I don't remember screaming, but apparently, I was. I do remember the doctor saying, "Somebody get this kid something for that damn pain."

And that's the last thing I remember.

I woke up post-surgery in a Methodist Hospital in Houston. They had cut off my big toe and part of the ball of my foot. Dr. Fein, a well-known orthopedic surgeon, did the procedure. He told my parents I would have balance issues and wouldn't walk right again. He was one of the best orthopedic surgeons in the country and had just performed surgery on Dan Pastorini, quarterback for the Houston Oilers. So, he was very good at what he did and knew what he was talking about. But he was wrong: two months later I made the eighth-grade basketball team as a seventh grader.

But the first day back to school after I lost my toe, I started out in a wheelchair. That lasted one day, and when I got home, I said, "I ain't doing that." So, it was crutches for the next three days. But that didn't work for me either. Crutches are incredibly limiting for a guy who only knows 100 miles an hour. About three weeks after surgery, I had cut the front of an old shoe out and wrapped up my foot so I could walk on it. Because the wound needed to heal from the inside out, they hadn't sewn it all the way up. So, in that first week, I went home several times a day to change the wrap.

And Doctor Fein was right, I didn't walk normally on it—for about six weeks. After that, I was fine. No physical therapy, I just learned how to walk on it. Two and a half months later, I was playing basketball, jumping, and stopping with no balance issues.

Was I in pain? Hell yeah, it was excruciating. Early on, when I stopped quickly and that newly formed skin rolled over that bone, I'd fall to the court in agony. It felt like somebody had shot me, and it hurt bad enough to take me down. The coach would come out, but by the time he reached me, the pain had subsided, and I was saying, "I'm fine. I'm fine." Then, I'd get up and go. I couldn't imagine anything stopping me from playing ball or riding my new motor bike.

So, Dad cut down the stump and I was back dirt biking within a month. And I was wearing the mandatory protective gear—most of the time.

A TALE OF TWO PARENTS

That first night in the hospital was rough for Mom. Not for me—I was out cold. I had been assigned to a room with a few other male patients and Mom wasn't allowed to visit. What can I say? It was the 70s in Texas.

She told the hospital staff, "I'm staying tomorrow night no matter what, so y'all better move him or do something because I'm staying." Mom's the kindest, gentlest woman on the planet unless you mess with one of her boys, then she'll tear you up. Which my sixth-grade teacher, Miss Little, discovered just a few weeks later.

I stayed in the hospital for a week, was home for another, and then back to school. Mom met with the principle to pass along the doctors' instructions. "I don't want him in a crowded locker room or hallway with all the kids because, if he bumps his foot, it can start bleeding again."

The principal said, "No problem. We'll let him leave class a few minutes early. That way he won't be in the hall with all the other kids."

Near the end of class on that first day back, I reminded my teacher, Miss Little, of the arrangement. "Ma'am, I'm supposed to leave before the bell."

Miss Little, likely raised by angry nuns in a previous century, had no tolerance for any form of impartiality. She looked at me and said, "Some of you kids have your parents come up here to get special treatment. You'll be dismissed when everybody else is." So, I left with the rest of the class. As you'd expect, I bumped my foot and it started bleeding.

The school called Mom because my bandage was soaked through with blood. Bill Hart, a local pharmacist and friend of Dad's, went to the office with Mom to meet the principal. As the story goes, they brought in Miss Little and Mom told her, "I don't care who you are. If this happens again, I promise you, I'm gonna whip your butt all over Tarkington Prairie!"

I left class early the next day and for weeks after.

You don't mess with Mom's boys! Not if you're a professional quarterback, a seventh-grade teacher, or a baseball umpire. As far as my mom is concerned, I only throw strikes. Dad couldn't sit with her at Joe's or my baseball games. And later, when I was playing in the Big Leagues, my wife didn't like sitting by her either for all the trouble she gave the umpires:

"You're not gonna sleep a minute tonight because you've slept the whole game."

"Pull the good eye out of your pocket."

"You couldn't make a call if you had a phone book!"

"Is your rule book written in braille?"

And my favorite, "Your mother wears tennis shoes to church."

She never cussed; she was way to creative for that.

If Mom was the gentle giant who loved me fiercely with a generous bias, Dad was the rock upon which I stood. But Dad could also
be the rock upon which I was broken. He came from a tough family.

Joe and I were close to Dad's mom, Nanny. She was a great lady.
She was strong and stern and didn't show a whole lot emotionally,
but she loved my brother and me. But when you hugged her she'd
pull away. Like I said, she was a tough lady. But she was tough for a
reason: she'd had a tough life.

Dad's father ran out on them when Dad was young and left
Nanny as well as four kids. So, Dad kind of raised himself. He was
a tough kid from the wrong side of the tracks, so to speak. When he
was about twelve years old, on Fridays, he'd hitchhike from Cleveland
to Liberty, which was twenty-six miles. He'd work the weekend at a
gas station and hitchhike back on Sundays. He built his first car at
fourteen with my uncle Sonny. Dad could (and still can) build pretty
much anything. He went to college for a year, but that wasn't for him.
So, he joined the Navy and was an aircraft mechanic on the USS Midway in the early 60s. He was tough going in and tougher coming out.

Then he met my mom. Talk about opposites.

My parents officially met at a football game. But Mom knew
about Dad before that. He had a reputation as a bit of a ruffian. Mom
lived in a little bitty house in town. Dad's best friend lived across the
street. Mom remembers seeing Dad pull up in the hot rod he'd built
and thinking he was a thug, a trouble-maker, a rapscallion. But years
later she found herself quite attracted to that hot rod driving fella.

Just out of the service, my dad took his mama—who was a foot-
ball person, like all Grimsleys—to Livingston for the football game.
They got there late and the stands were full. So, Dad and Nanny stood.
Mom was at that game, too. She had gone with her boyfriend's mother.
They also arrived late and stood. And apparently, Mom stood out.

Later that same night, after both Dad and Mom had ditched their adults, Mom went to the local drive-in, Darts. The way Mom tells it, "He was sitting there in his car, and when I pulled up, he got out of his car and into mine."

Actually, it was Mom's boyfriend's car, and he was away at college. But he wasn't her boyfriend for very long after the rough-but-confident Grimsley fella swooped in. They fell in love, got married, and started a family. Where Dad can be hard, stubborn, and stoic, Mom is gentle, generous, and kind. But they are both faithful, hardworking, and kind to each other.

Dad had several jobs in the early years. He rode broncs and roped calves, drove a bread truck, and then worked at a gas station. Then a man named Mr. Hawthorne of Hawthorne Welding in Cleveland took Dad under his wing and taught him how to weld. Dad excelled and provided a steady income for us after that, but he was gone a lot working on pipelines across the country.

Mom and Dad made a good team and provided a good home for my brother and me. Dad was rough but fair. He expected obedience and respect and hard work, and he'd whoop us if we didn't tow those lines. He was never cruel, just matter of fact. Growing up with him, I felt fear but it was born out of respect and admiration. I didn't want to mess up. He wasn't light handed with the belt and could be pretty harsh, but I always knew he loved me. Dad might not have voiced his love for me when I was younger but there was never a doubt in my mind that he loved me.

As I got older, I understood what he went through as a kid and young man and what he had to fight for to get to where he is today. I recognized the sacrifices that he made for us, for his family. Dad taught me how to work and not take shit from anybody. He taught me how to stand up for what's right. To this day he is, and always will be, my hero. But today, Dad has also become my friend, and there's nothing quite like that.

UNCLE CLARENCE

Dad got me my first gun—a 20 gauge Winchester single shot—and taught me how to shoot. But Dad was gone a lot growing up, so most of the time it was Papaw or Uncle Clarence who took us hunting. We hunted squirrel and rabbit at first, then bigger game.

I'm a better shot than my brother. That's not bragging, or at least, not just bragging; it's also further insight into how I'm wired. If I love something, I'm pretty focused on perfecting it. So, I don't miss much. Neither does Joe, but he subscribes to what we call ATV shooting: Accuracy Through Volume.

Every boy needs an Uncle Clarence, though. Uncle Clarence lived in a house behind ours. Joe and I would get up in the morning and walk over to his place. He'd make us breakfast and then take us hunting.

Squirrel hunting is fun; there's never a dull moment. The dogs chase the squirrels up the trees, then you shoot them. You're never waiting; you're always active and moving. We'd start in the morning and wouldn't stop until Uncle Clarence was out of beer. And that is how I learned to drive. I always say my uncle taught me to drive but not necessarily through instruction. Mostly I had to figure it out because he was three sheets to the wind by the time we headed home.

I might've been twelve the first time he gave me the keys. I got to drive his old '52 Chevy. Joe and I loaded Uncle Clarence into the passenger side of his truck. My ten-year-old brother helped me out by sitting on his knees so he could assist in scanning over the dash for obstacles. It was helpful, too, because I had all I could handle with the shifter, the clutch, and an unpowered steering wheel that spanned the length of my arms.

One day when we were almost home, his dog saw us coming and decided he'd get on the truck's running board. Uncle Clarence was hammered, and when he saw the dog, he opened his door to holler at the dog just as I turned into his driveway. *Wham!* Out went Uncle Clarence. Needless to say, he didn't feel a thing and was just a little scraped up. He was a piece of work, a good man; we loved him, and he loved us. And he was always up for hunting.

GET YOUR OWN BALL

When I was twelve, just after I lost my toe, I was playing basketball with my friends in the gym. A big kid named Matt—a fourteen-year-old who was supposed to be in the ninth grade but wasn't—walked over and took our basketball. We might as well have said, "Oh, well, I guess we're done playing ball.' My buddies just stood there, heads down.

But I was pissed. It wasn't right. Something had to be done. So, I went over, grabbed the ball, and said, "Get your own damn ball."

Of course, Matt couldn't let that pass. I remember he was wearing jeans and no shirt; he was all muscle and at least a foot taller than me. I knew I couldn't win. So before he could even say anything, I hit him in the mouth. It surprised him, but that's about all it did. He hit me three times and knocked me down.

For a moment he thought it was over, but I stood up and hit him in the mouth again. He hit me three more times, harder this time, and knocked me down. But I stood up and punched again. This happened two more times until finally, he stopped, turned, and walked away. I picked up the ball and walked back over to my friends.

Their eyes were huge and one of them said, "What's wrong with you?"

"What do you mean?" I asked.

"You got your butt whooped."

"Yeah, but I got the ball back, didn't I?"

Matt never bothered me again. Can't say the same for my friends.

I tell this story because it may best describe who I was as a kid and who I would become—fearless and willing to give and take to protect what was right and just. And this story also reveals a protective mechanism I developed at a very young age because I was molested by an older boy who lived down the road.

HIDDEN ABUSE

I chose to tell you this story at the end of the chapter. I did that so it wouldn't color my childhood in a negative light. I wanted you to get to know my family and me without having to hurdle the abuse. I had a great childhood—a wild and free and brilliant and rough and rowdy childhood. I was loved and challenged and protected and encouraged.

But it happened. I was abused for a few years, and it significantly impacted the next thirty, mostly because I hid it. I was forty-eight—a year removed from the attempt to kill myself—when I first shared about the abuse and began to understand the impact it had on me. I was young, and it was confusing. I knew something was wrong, but the abuse was presented as a game. Looking back, I realize how I looked up to the kid and didn't want to lose the friendship. I told myself I didn't mind it, that it was just a game.

Of course, it wasn't. I was a boy, and it was abuse.

Sadly, attached to that type of abuse was the shame of having done something wrong. And that shame imprisoned me and haunted me for the next thirty years. That shame played a role in shaping the tough guy, bad ass, never-back-down persona I would develop. I became a man who couldn't allow anything I did to be considered gay or effeminate or appear as vulnerable; vulnerability wasn't something I could participate in. I went to the other extreme. I was the man's man, the antithesis of somebody who could be abused. I'm talking, I went to the extreme: my idea was to punch first, and often. I couldn't show any weakness.

I don't hold anything against the kid that abused me. My guess is it was done to him as well. That's almost always the way of it. This is a broken world, and I've forgiven him.

I can also look back and see how God walked with me through the years in this broken world. I am now experiencing how God's love reconciles what was lost and restores what was taken. That's one of the reasons I wrote this book and why I want to be honest and vulnerable in it. You see, I have discovered that there is no condemnation or shame for those in Christ Jesus, that He is the Savior of this broken world. It's my hope that you might discover this as well. That's why I tell my story.

THE LONG GAME

When it comes to writing my story, it's not just my story: it's my parents' and grandparents' stories, and it's also about my kids and my grandkids. Family is the whole story. And I'm discovering that family is the long game; our heavenly Father is the long game. God is restoring and reconciling and redeeming and we are invited to trust.

My entire family still lives in Tarkington Prairie. Dana, the kids, and I go there as often as we can to visit Dad and Mom, and Joe and his wife, Lynn. We laugh and remember the good times, and we remind each other of our love for one another in the dark times.

I am still learning how family is the generational context that provides opportunity to love and forgive and wrestle down the truth that sets us free so that we might pass along that love, forgiveness, and freedom. I see the faithful wrestling of my grandparents and parents and of my wife and kids. And I'll spend the rest of this book writing about my own wrestling, in hopes that what I have discovered—and am still discovering—about the love of God will encourage you.

CHAPTER THREE

A Boy Becomes a Ballplayer

NINE DAYS

September 8, 1989

My feet never touched the turf as I walked out to the mound in my crisp new Phillies uniform. This was a dream realized—relief and excitement all packed into a single moment. "I knew I could do this," I thought. I felt excited, nervous, and proud all at the same time.

There were thirty thousand in attendance in Montreal, give or take a few. Tim Raines was the first to bat for the Expos. He hit a grounder and was thrown out at first. The next guy was Grissom. I threw three strikes, but the umpire was calling balls. I didn't know why, so I walked him. I faced Huson next—same thing. I threw three more pitches and three more strikes, but the umpire wasn't friendly. He was still calling balls, so Huson walked too. The next guy was Hubie Brooks—same thing. This was not good. I was sweating and breathing heavy. I'd gotten one out, walked three, and the bases were loaded.

Phillies pitching coach Darold Knowles—a guy I'd known all of one day—walked out to the mound. All I could think was, "Mom and Dad just bought tickets they couldn't afford to fly to Montreal.

They took their first plane ride ever to a country they've never been to so they could watch me get one out?!"

Darren Daulton, our catcher, joined Knowles, and they reached the mound at the same time. "What's going on?" Knowles asked. I shook my head, but before I could respond Darren barked, "I'll tell ya what the hell's going on: the kid's throwing strikes and this umpire is screwing him." By then the umpire had come over. Knowles turned and chewed on him a little bit. Hearing him, our manager, Nick Leyva, joined in from the dugout. My new team had my back, and I could feel it.

Then Darren looked back to home plate and nodded toward Andrés Galarraga, who was warming up to bat. Galarraga was leading the National League in home runs and RBIs. I was in a tight spot. A twenty-one-year-old kid in his Major League debut, one out, and bases loaded. And my catcher looks at me and says, "He likes fast balls, away."

I nodded, "Okay."

He spit. "I'm gonna set up on the outside half plate. I'm not even gonna give a sign. Just give it to me."

I was thinking, "You want me to throw fastballs to a fastball hitter—who's one of the best homerun hitters in the league—with the bases loaded? That's bold. I love it. Let's go!"

I nodded with a half-grin. "Okay." I threw the first pitch; he took it for a strike. I threw the next one, and he fouled it off. I struck him out on my fourth pitch. The next guy was Foley. He grounded out.

And I was in the paper the next day:

Jason Grimsley wins debut. Former Reading pitcher helps Phillies top Expos.

> Grimsley, in his first start since being called up by
> Philadelphia Tuesday, pitched five innings and won
> his major league debut as the Phillies beat Montreal
> 4-3 Friday night, dropping the Expos into fourth
> place in the National League East.
>
> Grimsley walked three straight batters with one
> out in the first, but escaped the bases loaded jam
> by striking out Galarraga and getting Tom Foley on
> a grounder.

I won my debut! Mom and Dad ended up sitting next to actor Donald Sutherland, who is a big Expos fan. We still have it on video: Mom, Dad, and Donald, watching me play my first big league game. He'd just wrapped a film called *A Dry White Season* with Susan Sarandon and Marlon Brando. Nice guy. Great actor. (Though I will forever picture him with his mouth wide open, eyes huge, pointing at the camera in *Invasion of the Body Snatchers*.)

And if you'd asked me 1,555 days earlier—we'll get to why this number is important in a minute—if I thought that someday I'd be pitching in front of thirty thousand people while Mom and Dad chummed it up with a co-star of Marlon Brando, I might have said, "Hell yeah!"

But if you'd asked me seven days before that, I'd have thought you were crazy. That's because the plan was never baseball. I wouldn't have imagined it even possible. It's amazing how God knows the desires of our hearts, walks beside us, and guides our paths—and what can change in nine days.

THE PERFECT SPORT

Throughout high school I played football, basketball, and baseball—

like everyone did back in those days. Sports in the 70s in East Texas was as much a religion as Christianity. There might've been fifty people at the Baptist church on Sunday, but there were five times that number Friday night at the football game. And it didn't matter your denomination, social standing, economic position, political stance, or skin color—everyone supported their ball players.

And in East Texas in the 70s, there were only three kinds of ball players: football, basketball, and baseball. I played all of them, religiously.

On special occasions like Easter or Christmas, you might find me with Mom and my brother at Mammaw's church, but every other day, my church was the basketball court, the football field, or the baseball diamond. And I attended with the zealous passion of a young convert. I loved everything about competing. I loved Friday nights: putting on the pads; the huddle; that moment before the snap, with every muscle tensed; and then the explosion of violence and control. I loved hitting and getting hit. I loved the heart-racing intensity of the basketball court too. Playing offense one moment and defense the next, blocking shots, the half-time buzzer, the coach's encouragement, the locker room celebrations when we won, and the common commiseration when we lost. But baseball was always the ultimate game for me, where my abilities thrived.

While platform shoes, shag carpet, disco, and *Star Wars* might have marked America in the 70s, America was best defined by baseball. And maybe nowhere more so than in the heart and mind of one East Texas kid who went by the name Jason Grimsley. To me, there is nothing more perfect than the game of baseball. Everything from the smell of fresh cut grass, the red clay, the chalk lines, the symmetry of the diamond, the intensity of the infield, the epic stakes of the outfield. Then there is the battle between pitcher and batter, the thrill of throwing one past the hitter. Win or lose, one pitch at a time over the course of nine innings, baseball is the perfect sport.

DASHED DREAMS?

I was seven years old when I started playing baseball. My first little league uniform was whatever tennis shoes we could find, blue jeans, and maroon shirts with Pace-Stancel Funeral Home written boldly across the front.

The funeral home is still there. Back then, Bubba Toller and Reggie Burrell owned and ran it. So, Bubba's daughter, Kim, played on the team. Dad was my first coach. And we had another kid named Brian Davis on the team. We called him Boo. No, not the blues musician, but he was pretty good at baseball. He ended up getting drafted and played for the White Sox in the minor leagues.

From the very beginning, I loved baseball. Morning till night, I wanted to throw the ball. I'd play catch with anyone. But by the time I was twelve, most people would not play catch with me, their complaint being: "You throw too hard." When I was fifteen, Dad stopped playing with me for the same reason. Maybe I could have taken some heat off the ball, but that thought never crossed my mind. I threw it hard because that's why God created baseballs and boys to throw 'em. 100 miles an hour or nothing—that's all I've ever known.

When I was still in Little League playing with the Ben Franklin Padres, Papaw came to watch me play. I pitched that day, and when he saw my pitch he said to my mom, "Judy, that boy is gonna play in the big leagues one day." Mom responded with a generously dismissive, "Oh, Daddy." She thought he was just saying what grandpas say. But when she tells that story now, it's with a twinkle in her eye, and a "He knew something, didn't he?" tone of voice. But I never heard that story until years later.

When I was a kid, playing in the big leagues was about as plausible as becoming a NASA astronaut and flying to the moon. It's not that I wouldn't have wanted to be a pro ball player, it just wasn't in my vocabulary. Just watching a big-league game was hard in Tarkington. We had a TV that got one channel, so if we were lucky, we might catch a game. But there wasn't more than one a week, and for longer than for most Americans, we couldn't watch in color.

I especially loved watching Nolan Ryan play. He was my hero. He was from Alvin, Texas—not that far from us. My grandfather on my dad's side had run a little restaurant and bar in Alvin for a time, and Nolan visited there. My dad remembered the name. So, when I watched Ryan play, I felt like I had a connection. And a VHS tape of him pitching, wore that sucker out.

So, as a kid, like most Texas boys—hell, like most American boys who grew up in the 70s—I fantasized about playing pro ball. But it was the typical fantasies of childhood. You know, the kind where you watch the boy in the back yard throwing a ball up and catching it and rolling on the ground, all the while talking to himself in an announcer's voice about how "the crowd goes wild."

I imagined it was the World Series in Yankee Stadium. I was wearing the blue and white pinstripes; it was bottom of the ninth in game seven. I was catching a bases-loaded fly ball, hitting the grand slam walk off, or pitching a no hitter.

But those were just childhood fantasies. By the time I was in high school, I played for the love of competing, the love of being a part of a team, the love of the game, and the love of winning. I had no real thoughts of going pro. It was such a ridiculous impossibility that I never even knew I could have dreamt it.

I did have a dream, though. My dad was an aircraft mechanic on the USS Midway. My grandfather and my uncles were Marines. My great uncle was a naval aviator who was killed in a plane crash while he was in the Navy. And my dream was the Air Force.

I was actually pretty smart for a redneck from East Texas. As Mom says, "Jason was good at school, and he could have been a valedictorian if he ever brought a book home."

I graduated toward the top of my class and got accepted on an academic scholarship to the Air Force Academy. And that was the plan. And not just a *plan*, that was the *dream*. I could see my whole future laid out and I was excited about it.

Just before graduating—I'm talking days—the military rep came to meet with me, only to inform me that I had failed the physical. He said, "Due to your medical history, we can't take you." It was like he was speaking Greek. I don't speak Greek. "What medical history?" I thought.

I assumed it had something to do with the Air Force and so I said, "That's okay, I'll just go into another branch."

He looked at me seriously and said, "No, son, because of the foot injury you sustained as a kid, you're 4F; you're physically unfit to serve in the military. No branch is gonna take you."

Physically unfit? It was like a fist to the jaw. I couldn't get my head around the idea that a lost toe exempted me. Outside of a lot of pain and a little shared trauma with Mom, it hadn't impacted any part of my life since. I tried to tell him that. It didn't matter. My dream was shattered. I had no idea what I was going to do.

But my baseball coach, Rick Lynch, he had an idea.

It's amazing just how quickly everything can change. In a moment, the desires of your heart—maybe even the desires you weren't aware of, or had kept hidden, or told yourself were impossible, or the fantasies of childhood—are suddenly right in front of you, there for the taking.

TRY OUTS

The year before, I pitched one game. It was against Livingston High School. We played them before district games started. They were a 4-A school, and we were 3-A—a small-town team. We weren't expected to win.

I went out and stuck it up their rear. I pitched a really good game and we won. Looking back, that game may have been the most significant I ever pitched. Not because it was one of the best games I ever pitched, not even close. And not because it was a big game—it was just two Texas high school teams playing the first in a season of many. And not because lots of people saw it; hardly anyone saw it.

It may have been the most significant game I ever pitched because Rick Lynch saw it. Rick Lynch was the head coach of the other team, and he watched me pitch what would turn out to be the last game I pitched in high school.

The next week, while doing speed drills on tackling dummies in offseason spring football, a lineman named Keith More stumbled in front of me. I put my hand up as I was flying through and snapped my right wrist, breaking both bones. The doctor in Cleveland should have pinned it but didn't. Four weeks later, they had to rebreak and reset it. The whole season was lost.

Then, in my senior year, coach Rick Lynch moved to Tarkington Prairie as the linebackers coach. His dad, Tom Lynch, was the head coach of the Tarkington Prairie High School football team. Rick also took over coaching the baseball team and was excited to have me pitch for him in my senior year. But in the last game of basketball season, I got my legs cut out from under me and went down hard. I broke my left wrist and hurt my right shoulder. I didn't get to pitch my senior year, either.

Looking back, if I'd pitched those last two years in high school, I might have considered the possibility of dreaming about going further in baseball. Who knows? Instead, my future plans only included a military career and I dreamed about it often.

Until the day that dream was shattered.

When I got back to my house around 9 p.m. on the night I graduated, Coach Lynch was waiting for me. He told my parents he wanted to borrow me for a few days. We ended up leaving Tarkington Prairie around 11:30 that night. We drove all night and arrived in Arlington around 5 the next morning. We got a hotel room, signed in, and then headed straight over to the field where the Philadelphia Phillies were holding a tryout which started at 7 that morning.

I walked with coach Lynch as we made our way to the Phillies' scout, Doug Gassaway.

"Doug, good to see ya. Listen, we drove all night and got in at 5 a.m. Can Jason come back tomorrow?"

Doug looked at me briefly. I was six foot tall, stick thin, maybe weighed 150 pounds, and still had braces. I was seventeen but looked fourteen. Doug smiled, looked back to Coach, and replied, "If you don't mind him facing the guys we want to take a second look at, it's fine with me."

"Na, we don't mind," Coach said. We went back to the hotel room and got some rest. Then, we got up bright and early the next day so I could throw a baseball.

At the tryout, the players stretched as a group and played catch in the outfield. I was told I'd be pitching second. So, as the first pitcher headed to the turtle—that portable batting practice backstop that is erected behind home plate—I headed to the bullpen to warm up.

The catcher—a guy who played for the University of Texas at Arlington—who was already in the bullpen, looked at me strangely. In hindsight, I think my presence confused him. He probably wondered why a fourteen-year-old was in his bullpen.

"What are you doing?" he asked.

I nodded toward the field. "I'm gonna throw," I said matter-of-factly, clueless of my appearance.

He looked at me dismissively, nodded, and said, "Alright." Then we played a little catch. Then he asked, "You ready?"

"Yep."

He nodded again, pulled down his mask and got down into a squat. "Alright."

I picked up my leg and turned it loose. It went right by his glove and hit the screen behind him. He started laughing and shaking his head. I didn't know why he was laughing, but I threw a few more. Then it was time.

As we were walking onto the field he said, "I'd tell you good luck, but you don't need it."

"What?" I asked, confused.

He grinned, shook his head, and said, "Nothing." Then he turned for home plate.

As I headed to the mound, Doug Gassaway, who was standing behind the hitting screen, called out to me, "What's your name?"

"Jason Grimsley."

Coach Lynch and at least ten college coaches were standing off to the side. They glanced at me and then all but Coach went back to talking. Nobody was paying attention; no one seemed interested in watching a fourteen-year-old pitch.

The catcher got ready. I stepped onto the mound, warmed up with a few tosses, then I picked my leg up and threw. When the ball hit the catcher's glove, it sounded like a gun had gone off. Everybody's head snapped up at the sound.

I could see Gassaway talking to the catcher, who had taken his mask off and was laughing and nodding. Then he pulled his mask back down and threw me the ball. I got back on the mound and looked up. Now there were at least ten radar guns pointed in my direction. All eyes were fixed on me.

I threw the next one, and before it even got to the catcher, Gassaway was strutting toward me shouting, "Hey, son, where the hell have you been?"

Then he stood behind me while I faced the next five hitters. Four strike outs with only one guy fouling off. I threw around 93 miles per hour—way better than anyone there expected. I left the mound only to be greeted by a gaggle of enthusiastic coaches who wanted to know my story, where I was from, and how long I'd played ball. I could see Coach Lynch behind them, grinning.

Before the day was done, Coach Lloyd Simmons of Seminole Junior College asked me to play for him. Seminole had won the Junior College World Series a few times; they were a powerhouse in JUCO baseball. And just like that, I had a new dream. Or maybe I was finally empowered to dream in a new way, because it was more like I awakened to what I had always dreamed.

It was just a spark of a possibility, but it was enough. A spark can start a hell of a fire.

Days earlier I had been denied the military future I had dreamed of and just a few days later, I could play baseball. And it wasn't a consolation; it was an elevation.

Things happened fast after that tryout.

On June 6, before I could even play for Seminole Junior College, I got a Western Union telegram telling me I'd been drafted by the Philadelphia Phillies in the tenth round, 252nd overall. I had gone from not knowing what I was gonna do on May 28 to being drafted to play professional baseball on June 6.

Seven days.

And on June 8, Doug Gassaway and another scout showed up at the house with a contract to play rookie ball for the Phillies A-team in Bend, Oregon. And they were looking for me to sign it.

THEN GO PLAY BALL, SON

If everything that happened was excitingly fast for me, it was devastatingly fast for the women in my life. We all sat around the kitchen table discussing my future. I'd never been away from home, and suddenly I was propositioned to play for the Phillies Rookie ball team in Oregon. Mom and my grandmothers were adamantly against it.

"No." Mom spoke the word with force while both of my grandmothers nodded in emphatic agreement. So, it was pretty tense in the room when I looked at my dad for some advice. And boy, did he have it.

"Son, for seventeen years I've clothed and fed you and put a roof over your head. In those seventeen years, I hope I've instilled the values you need to make this decision. 'Cause, son, I can't make it, your mom can't make it, your grandmothers can't make it, the scouts can't make it. You gotta make it. What do you want to do?"

The answer came quick. "I want to play ball."

Dad smiled, nodded. "Then go play ball, son."

My dad's words were a powerful sustaining force. He hadn't just given me permission; he'd given me his blessing. "I believe in you, son!" was expressed and felt in every nuance of that interaction. I don't think my grandmother talked to him for a month, and she didn't talk to my high school coach for almost a year. She was so mad. She did not want me to leave.

But a few days later, my family walked me to the Houston airline gate (something you could do back then), hugged me, and waved as

I boarded my first commercial flight. They waited until the plane was out of sight. Mom bawled.

ONE THOUSAND, FIVE HUNDRED, FIFTY-FIVE DAYS

Approximately three and a half years later, or exactly 1,555 days from when I signed my contract (if you're counting), I took the mound in Montreal in front of my parents, Donald Sutherland, and 30,000 fans, give or take, to pitch my first win for the Philadelphia Phillies in the Major Leagues.

Everything in my life changed in nine days; in a moment, the opportunity of a lifetime was in front of me. But it took 1,555 days to make it happen. In a moment, you can find yourself with an incredible opportunity—but it's just an opportunity. I think life is about what we do with those opportunities and what we discover along the way.

This life is a journey of chasing down, defining, and redefining.

Even though I was unaware of God's closeness in those days, I can look back and see His footprints next to mine and recognize the evidence of His love for me. It's amazing how God knows us and guides us—even when we don't know Him. And it's amazing how He gives us people who champion and encourage us along the way.

From the confidence-instilling "Then go play ball, son" of my dad, to the off seasons I spent living with Rick and Nancy Lynch and their encouragement, to the workouts Rick provided at my old high school before each spring training, to the encouragement of my family and community as Tarkington Prairie's own—I was confident I would make the big leagues.

ROOKIE BALL

There are many levels in minor league baseball; several developmental rungs on the ladder to playing in the Major Leagues, including Rookie ball, Short Season-A, A-Ball, Double-A, and Triple-A.

If you're a polished college kid who's just been drafted, you might go to a Double-A or even a Triple-A team where you're only a rung or two from the possibility of being pulled up onto the Major League team. But when you get drafted straight out of high school and are a complete unknown, like I was, Rookie ball is where you start.

The Phillies put me on the bottom rung playing for their farm team in Bend, Oregon. And I couldn't have been happier or more confident. I'm not sure where it came from, but I had a confidence that couldn't be dissuaded. Oregon was simply the first step on my way to playing pro ball. Period.

I left home awakened to the real possibility of playing the game I loved for a living. I had an opportunity to chase a childhood dream I never even imagined possible. I took on the next weeks, months, and years with a no-looking-back attitude. Call it the ignorance of youth or some inner drive, but I felt fully confident that I was on the road to a pro career.

So, while Mom cried, I got on my first commercial flight, all nerves and bold excitement. I flew from Houston to Portland, then took a puddle jumper to northwest Oregon where I waited at the arrivals area of the airport for somebody from the team to pick me up. Nobody came.

Looking back, it was a good way to start my baseball career. I picked up on an essential maxim in pro ball: no one is gonna hand me anything. I alone determine my value.

A fella with a van noticed I was waiting around and asked where I was headed. "I'm here to play ball," I told him. He looked at me good-naturedly, then shrugged.

"I know where you're going, hop in." He drove me to the ballpark. Nice guy.

When I got there, I told the gatekeeper, "I'm here to play ball." He looked at me funny, kinda like the pitcher at my tryouts. He didn't believe me and wouldn't let me in. But I insisted until he got the manager, PJ Carrie.

"Yeah, he's one of mine," Carrie said.

It felt great to say it, and it was true: "I'm here to play ball." And I had one goal: to make it to the Major Leagues.

I remember PJ Carrie's first talk to the team. "Boys, I want you to look around the locker room. One of you, maybe two of you, will get into the big leagues. That's just the way it is."

And I kid you not, what went through my head was, "Alright, who's the other one?"

There were approximately twenty-two players on our baseball team at any moment. Most of them had already played a season or two of Rookie or college ball. So, they were in their early twenties and more experienced. I was one of three seventeen-year-olds. And though I still looked fourteen, I was confident I would make it.

Looking back on that team, Coach wasn't far off—four of us made it to the big leagues. By no stretch of the imagination was I the most talented individual there and I knew it. But it didn't matter. I knew I was gonna play in the big leagues.

I think my confidence came from three things. First, I wanted to make it just a little more than the other kids. Second, I've never been afraid of hard work. That cliché you often hear a coach use during an interview to describe a player's dedication—"first into the building, last out"—was me. I was willing to work harder than everybody else, and I knew how to work. All that hay bailing and post digging in my summers paid off.

Third, and this is pretty important, I loved it. I absolutely loved baseball. I loved practicing, the idea that I could get better, being on a team, game day, competition. I loved wining and even loved the chip on my shoulder when we lost.

I loved

everything

about

the game.

That means I was willing to put up with all the outside stuff that came with playing on a Rookie ball team. The kind of stuff that might have worn out other kids. And there's a bunch of it.

I was told I'd be staying at a Holiday Inn. It was the Holiday Motel—there's a big difference. Six of us lived in a two-bedroom suite. Outside of travel games, I don't think I slept on an actual mattress until three years later when I got called up.

And then there was all the stuff that comes with being a grown up. Suddenly I had to wash my clothes, buy my own toiletries, and feed myself. I was making $238 every two weeks. I learned quickly that ramen noodles and peanut butter go a long way. $12,500. That's what they gave me to sign. I was so happy! I was getting paid to play ball! I couldn't sign my first contract because I was still a minor—playing in the Minors. My dad had to because Mom wouldn't sign it. I played the full three-month Short Season-A. It was a whirl of practices, games, laundry, and ramen.

The next year I went to Spring Training along with one hundred other Phillies developmental players, then back to Short Season-A. It was the same level, Rookie ball, but a different club. The Phillies had two Rookie ball teams. The other was in Utica, NY. That's where I played the 1986 baseball season, my second in the Minor Leagues.

I was still on the bottom rung, still had the same odds of making the Major Leagues, still felt the same love of the game, and still held the same unshakable confidence.

STAYING CONFIDENT

The main reason I was still throwing on a Rookie ball team was no secret. I couldn't throw a strike to save my life. I could throw the ball through a wall; I just didn't know what wall I was gonna hit.

I remember playing a scrimmage game that second year where I think I'd thrown 99 pitches in two innings. For new baseball fans, that's way too many pitches. At some point in the third inning, Robin Roberts—a former MLB pitcher and Hall of Famer—stormed onto the field. Robin was the Phillies' Minor League pitching director at the time. He wasn't wearing a uniform, he wasn't coaching, and he had no business being on the field, but there he was in his street clothes coming at me. And he was yelling "Timeout!" as he approached the mound. At first, I hoped he was just gonna give me some advice or encouragement; I sure as hell could've used some. Instead, he barked out in frustration, "Grims, you're horseshit! This is embarrassing. You need to quit and go home!"

Now remember, I was an eighteen-year-old kid in the middle of the field, fully aware I wasn't anywhere close to throwing strikes. This could have been devastating for me except, before I could even register what Roberts was saying, my manager, Tony Taylor started yelling. Because it was a scrimmage, Tony was on the field behind me acting as umpire. He'd watched Robin storm his field and address his pitcher, and he was livid.

Tony was one of the first, if not the first, Cuban-born players in the big leagues. He knew how to overcome odds, and he understood good coaching. Before the last word was out of Roberts' mouth, in broken English Tony unloaded, "You don't listen to that #&$ksucker

mother fucker. He don't throw hard. You throw hard. One day you throw strikes. Fuck him. You throw the ball; we'll teach you to throw strikes. Fuck him!"

Roberts was a hall of famer. His words could've left a mark, could've rattled my confidence, but Tony sticking up for me is what ended up leaving the mark. That whole year, Tony stuck up for me. And I needed it. I struggled. I led the league in walks and losses that year. I was 1-10. But the one win I threw was a 9-inning shutout.

And it was enough. The next year I went to Spartanburg, South Carolina.

Still confident—not certain, never that—I was good enough, confident I'd outwork everyone again.

SUCCESS AND FAILURE

Pat Combs is a good friend. Pat manages my finances and gives me advice. He's killed it in finance, but I met him playing baseball. Pat was a left hander. Left-handed pitchers are a little screwy. Pat's a little screwy. Almost killed me with a shotgun when he accidently pulled the trigger while we were duck hunting. It was on his shoulder and near my head.

Pat played in Houston in high school and had a ton of success. He went to Baylor, where he may have lost five games the whole time he was there. He played on the US Olympic team in '88 and was drafted by the Phillies the same year as me. Except he was a first rounder. He went to the Florida State League for a minute, then Double-A. The next year I went to Double-A and Pat went Triple-A. Then, at the end of that season, we both got called up to the Major Leagues at the same time.

In his first games he went 4-0 against teams like the Mets and the Cardinals. Both of those teams were in the hunt, and Pat just shoved it up their asses. He was the man. Meanwhile, I won my debut then lost my next three. I got my ass handed to me. The next year, Pat started out in the bigs, I started out in Triple-A. Eventually I got called up and went 3-1 with the Phillies.

In his rookie year Pat was 10-10, not bad for a twenty-two-year-old kid. Hell, he won ten ball games as a rookie! But to Pat, there was a problem. You see, Pat had never lost ten ball games. So, in Pat's mind, there must've been something wrong. He started to change things, tried to fix things, and along the way lost confidence in himself. A few years later, he was done playing ball. Pat will be the first to tell you now that the problem wasn't with his ability or effort, it was that he'd equated losing with failure.

There's a difference between losing and failure. Losing has to do with the score, failing has to do with the effort. Failure is when you didn't do everything possible before and during the game. Failure is going half-assed. That was not Pat's problem. In a game that keeps track of every number and where those who watch determine success and failure by keeping track of those numbers, it's hard for an athlete not to do the same thing.

I had an advantage over Pat. I wouldn't have called it that at the time, but it's true. You see, I knew how to lose. I was a tenth-round pick, and I'd lost plenty of games. I was the 25th man on a twenty-five-man roster, so I learned quickly that if I was gonna make it in the big leagues, I couldn't base my success on wins or loses. Wins and losses were outside my control. What I could control was my effort, how I practiced, how I prepared, how I trained, how I focused.

And I could control my faith. I'm not talking about faith in God but faith in myself. If you lose faith in yourself or your ability, you're not long for competitive sport. Success for an athlete, and everyone else for that matter, is defined by two things: effort and not losing faith.

Because every freaking day, you fail and succeed, fail and succeed, fail and succeed, fail and succeed. And in pro sports, that emotional rollercoaster is what weeds out most athletes.

Talent is important, but I can tell you it's not all about talent. It's about learning how to navigate the emotional grind of winning and losing, bliss and despair; it's also about learning how to stay even and to not determine your worth or ability based on wins or losses.

"You can't get too high or too low." Every athlete says it, but the ones for whom it's true have a good shot at making it. It took me a while to figure that out, but when I did, my career really took off. I played twenty-two years. I was always the last man to make the roster, but I made plenty of rosters, played in some of the biggest games, and got my share of wins.

LET'S TALK ABOUT PITCHING

Asking a pitcher how they learned to pitch is like asking a comedian where they get their ideas. We just do it, have always been able to do it, and have no idea how we do it. I can tell you that our coaches taught us about a balance point, but it never really made much sense to me. They taught us to jerk the front side, but the guys who threw hard, they never jerked the front side. Plus, in those days, we didn't have the luxury of three-hundred-frames-per-second cameras to help us study our mechanics. That didn't come around until the late 90s or early 2000s. So, you couldn't really study yourself anyway.

There was certainly a handful of coaches who helped me in those early years. Dan Warthen, my first coach in Bend; George Culver; Jim Wright; Bob Tiefenhour; and Mike Willis. These guys were all great encouragers who were patient with me through trial and error.

Here's what I can tell you about pitching: First, you can't teach fast, you either are or you're not. Second, it's all about trial and error. Third, repetition. That's pretty much it. This all started falling into place in year three when I was playing in Clearwater, Florida. I'll never forget. We were in Miami, playing downtown in Municipal Stadium. It's a rough neighborhood. During the game, we heard gunshots. It was a day game, and there might have been twelve people there; eleven of them were scouts.

And I just found it. I was finally pitching up to my ability. I got called up again, this time to the Double-A team in Redding, Pennsylvania. That's where I started out my fourth season. I was now pitching in a league that sits just under the Majors. So, I was twenty years old and going into Double-A. At the end of July, I was 6-10 with a three something Earned Run Average (ERA), which wasn't bad. August rolled around, and I went 5-0 through the month with a .5 ERA.

I was killing it. I was confident, I was loving it. And that's when I got called up to the big leagues—the Phillies!

ONE OF THE BEST PHONE CALLS OF MY LIFE

September 3, 1989

We had just lost to the Yankees Double-A team in the first round of the playoffs in the Eastern League. Our team was on the bus, headed home to Reading, Pennsylvania. The manager, Mike Hart, stopped at a rest area, got on a pay phone (there were no cell phones then), got back on the bus, looked at me, then sat down.

When we got back to Reading, I was headed into the clubhouse when Mike said, "Jason, I need to see you in the office."

I walked into the office, and before I could sit down, Mike said, "Talked to the Phillies. You're starting September 8 against Montreal." I couldn't believe it. I could totally believe it.

Mike waited till it sunk in. "Do you need to make a phone call?"

I smiled. "Yes sir, I do." I called the house. Mom answered.

"Mom, I need to talk to Dad."

"Is everything okay?"

"Yeah Mom, but I need to talk to Dad."

"Jason, what's wrong?"

"Mom! Nothing's wrong. Can I talk to Dad?"

She put Dad on the phone. "Everything all right?" he asked.

"Yep. Hey, what are you all doing on September 8th?"

"I'm going to work."

"No sir, you and Mom need to figure out a way to get to Montreal because I'm starting against the Expos."

There was a pause on the other end. Then, in the background, I heard Mom saying, "Oh my God, Johnny, what's wrong?"

I saw my dad cry one time—when Mom's dad died and Mom didn't want them to take the casket away. And he cried when I told him I'd made the Major Leagues.

"What do you want to do?" He'd asked me at a kitchen table a few years earlier.

"I want to play ball, Dad." The answer had come quick.

"Then go play ball, son." He'd said it and those words had sustained me.

Dad and Mom made it up to Canada to watch the game. I got them the family pass, so they had tickets right down front. Approximately three and a half years later, or exactly 1,555 days after Dad said, "Then go play ball, son," I took the mound in Montreal in front of my parents, Donald Sutherland, and about 30,000 fans to pitch the first of many wins.

It was a dream come true.

CHAPTER FOUR

The Man and His Reputation

YOU DIDN'T TELL ME NOT TO

In the 80s and 90s in the culture of baseball, there was a commonly agreed upon modus operandi where hooligans from East Texas could play the game just on the fringe of lawlessness. There was room within the game to get rowdy. And the fans loved it. In the 80s hockey wasn't the only sport where you went to a fight and a game broke out… baseball had its own share of fisticuffs.

Fact is, any sport played at its highest level is bound to develop a combative subculture; egos, testosterone, and elite competition are an explosive combination. But in the hypocrisy of today's cancel culture, a culture that rightly preaches tolerance and is intolerant with anyone who disagrees with whatever groupthink movement is in vogue, athletes and organizations are more careful with the optics.

So, while there's still plenty of ego, testosterone, and fighting in baseball, it's not a good idea to act like you enjoy it. And it's definitely not a good idea to acknowledge that a player or organization plans to fight. But in 1985, we planned it, kind of.

When I arrived in Bend, Oregon at the age of seventeen, I was introduced to the plastic batter, a plastic cut-out of a batter put in the box to help us practice pitch placement. But also, so you could practice how and where to hit the batter. I imagine teams have some modern version of the plastic batter today, but nobody's gonna admit to practicing how and where to hit it.

That same year, in my first team meeting, the one where our manager, PJ Carrie, told us only one or two would make it into the Major Leagues, he also said, "Gentlemen, I don't care what round you were drafted in. I don't care how big a prospect you are. If something happens and we get into a fight on the field and you don't go out there, we will release you."

I nodded and thought, "Obviously." This made perfect sense to me. It's the obvious and only option if you're gonna call yourself a teammate. But PJ should have been more specific, 'cause I was the kid from East Texas who participated in Fight Club every day after school in the grocery store parking lot next to Sonic, who punched first and asked questions later. So, the first time there was a scuffle I went running onto the field looking to throw blows. I grabbed the first guy not wearing my uniform and straight up cold cocked him. I ended up getting thrown out of that game. The first of many.

PJ came into the locker room hollering at me, "Son, what the hell are you doing?"

"PJ, you told us if we didn't go out there, you were gonna release us," I said, completely confused.

"I didn't tell you to hit nobody!" he said, matching my confusion.

"You didn't tell me not to."

A GOOD TEAMMATE

For me, fighting was a part of life, a certainty that couldn't be avoided. It was also part of the game, and as a younger man, part of the fun.

And in the 80s and 90s there was room for it in baseball. But if it was mostly accepted within the limits of the game, like always, I pushed the limits. And eventually, over the course of my career, I developed a reputation for two things: I was one hell of a teammate, and I was not a man to be messed with. Of course, I took great pride in both.

If you were on my team, then on or off the field, I had your back; loyalty was a huge deal to me, and still is. There's nothing worse than a teammate who doesn't have your back. I remember one night in a club after a game I saw a bunch of hotheads being disrespectful to a waitress. I was there with a few teammates and one, who will go unnamed, was next to me when I noticed the injustice. He'd also noticed and agreed with me that they needed to be confronted.

"Whatever happens, don't let that guy sucker punch me," I said, nodding to the guy closest to him as we walked over. My teammate nodded back, "I got him."

I confronted the dick lily who had been acting the fool, but before he even responded I was suddenly stumbling and discombobulated. Why? Because "that guy" I'd highlighted to my teammate on the way over had sucker punched me across the side of my head. Confused, I looked back for my teammate; he was running out the door. He'd done the worst thing a teammate could do. There's no greater insult or sin than bailing on a fella, especially just before trouble.

"That son of a bitch," I thought as I prepared myself for a beating. Then Jeff Grotewald, another teammate who had been watching the altercation from the second-floor balcony, defined what a teammate is with a magnificent display. Jeff did a Peter Pan off the second-floor landing onto the guy who'd hit me. Jeff and I are friends to this day. The guy who bolted? Not so much.

I often tell that story when describing what it means to me to be a teammate or friend—a brother. A guy who has your back when you're in a foxhole? That's someone you can trust. And the opposite is true: if you leave a teammate in a fight, you've lost all my respect.

I am learning a lot more about God's thoughts on being a teammate and friend. I think it has everything to do with how He never leaves us, especially when there's trouble. He's always had my back. Now I'm not suggesting He's all about ego, testosterone, and punching first. Like I said, I'm learning!

Anyway, while I never leapt off a second-floor balcony, it's the kind of thing I'd do if it was the only way to have a teammate's back. And everyone who called me a teammate knew it. I had a reputation as a guy who'd go through a brick wall for his teammates. I was a good teammate because I never left anyone in a bind. I would have literally taken a beating for someone before leaving them, though I much preferred to give beatings.

This leads to the second thing I was known for: I was not a man to be messed with.

NOT TO BE MESSED WITH

In the world of competition, when you're a part of a team, you are for each other. Also, you're against everyone else. Having a common enemy is one of the best ways to develop a sense of comradery and unified vision. It's us and them, good and evil, for and against, and it's awesome in competitive sports. (Not so much when the church does it, but I digress.)

You can develop quite the bond when it's us against the world. And so, in baseball, when it came to other teams, we hated them. All of them. But for reasons I never figured out through every level of the Minor Leagues, no matter who I played for, we especially hated the Red Sox, the Yankees, and the Tigers. This meant that in just about every series we played, there was almost always a moment when both teams would empty their respective dugouts for an all-out rumble at the pitcher's mound. Like I said, there's not as much fighting in baseball these days, but it happened a lot back then.

Well, in 1990 I was with the Phillies in Triple-A. It was after my debut in '89. We are playing the Pawtucket, Rhode Island Red Sox. Dana Kicker was pitching for them, and we had a guy named Dave Holland hitting. Dave is a big guy and could carry his weight in a big way. He's one of those guys you want in a foxhole. No doubt about it.

For some reason Dana decided to hit Dave. Dave is no plastic hitter, so he charged the mound. Of course, I ran onto the field. Except I hadn't pitched yet, so I knew I couldn't get kicked out. As I entered the melee, I said to myself, "I'm not going out here to hit nobody, I'm just gonna go be nice."

So, I grabbed a player and was pulling him off the pile when somebody put me in a choke hold and took me to the ground. It was like a switch flipped, and suddenly I went from Mr. Nice Guy, Jason Grimsley, to Jason Borne. "Whoever this is, I'm gonna beat the shit out of him," I thought. And screaming just below my consciousness was a thought I'd verbalize years later, after another altercation: "Nobody touches me that way!" I wasn't emotional—it was just a matter of fact.

He had a hold of me from behind, so I tucked my chin, held on to his arm, and pulled him over the top of me onto the ground. I threw my fist and hit him in the ear. His hat flew off revealing a head of gray hair, but I just kept at him. I was wearing out the right side of his head, just beating him into the ground.

At some point their trainer caught my arm and yelled, "Stop hitting him, stop hitting him!"

As they pulled me off, I was about to kick him in the face. And that's when I recognized it was Butch Hobson, the manager of the Red Sox. I remember him on the ground, looking at me, his face a mix of fear and confusion. Suffice to say, I didn't end up pitching in that game. But when it came to the league's perception of Jason Grimsley, my pitching had a lesser impact on my reputation than that fight.

I got back to the hotel and called Mom—I called her almost every night, still do—and she answered the phone by yelling at me.

"Jason! What are you doing? What were you thinking?"

"Ma'am?"

"You're all over the TV!"

"What?"

It turns out the Major League Boston Red Sox team had also had a bench-clearing, all-out Armageddon that night in their game. After ESPN showed the footage of the fight the analyst said, "And now, back on the farm," and the video cut to me beating the shit out of Butch.

"It looks like you grabbed a player, and he took exception to it," an interviewer noted to Butch Hobson in a post-game interview.

Butch nodded tiredly, "Yeah, I'm getting too old for this."

Mom was not happy about my fighting; she didn't like it at all. But I loved it—everything about it. This was the beginning of a reputation I continued to develop and take pride in over the rest of my career. Jason Grimsley was not a man to be messed with. And that reputation only grew when I started training with a guy named Gus Hoefling.

SIL-LUM KUNG FU

Gus was the strength and conditioning coach for the Philadelphia Phillies when I got to Major League camp in 1989. He'd been with them since the late 70s. And before that, well, that's the stuff of legends.

He was special forces before there was special forces. He served in in the Korean War and saw some shit. After, as the story goes, he walked into a California school of kung fu run by a man named Ed

Parker. Ed taught a form of martial arts called Kenpo, which is based on using knowledge of motion and logic as well as practicality and was designed to help defend against common modern modes of street-fighting.[8]

Gus ended up running a dojo for Ed and one day a small guy walked into his place with a mutual friend. Gus noticed he hadn't taken his shoes off and was affronted. As the story goes, after the fella declined Gus's demand to remove his shoes, Gus took matters into his own hands. He ended up thrown into a corner of the room. "I wasn't ready," Gus said.

The little guy nodded and said, "Same move, same corner." And then put Gus back in the same corner.

So, Gus, beaten twice, stood up and said, "Alright, when do we start training."

Gus left Ed and the dojo, got a job with the Flying Tigers Cargo Company, ended up in China, where he continued his training.[9] Eventually Gus came home to run a chain of gyms in Southern California, Arizona, and Nevada. In these gyms he developed a physical strength, conditioning, and flexibility program based on exercise theories from martial arts. This is how he met and started training Roman Gabriel, quarterback for the Los Angeles Rams from '62 to '72. When Gabriel was traded to the Eagles in '73, Gus went with him and ended up making a home in the City of Brotherly Love, where he ultimately ended up as the strength and conditioning coach for the Phillies.[10]

By the time I met Gus, he'd worked with greats like Steve Zable, Bill Bradley, Jerry Koosman, and Steve Carlton, who was arguably the best left-handed pitcher to ever play the game. Carlton is a Hall of Famer who still has the most strikeouts for a left-handed pitcher and is fourth all time behind Nolan Ryan, Randy Johnson, and Roger

Clemens. I absolutely loved everything about Gus. I loved the way he talked to me, challenged, motivated, and believed in me. He was no-nonsense but fun to be around. We developed a friendship.

When I got into baseball, it was frowned upon for pitchers to go into the weight room. We were basically told not to because it might throw off our motion or mechanics. But Gus's training went beyond the weight room. There was something unusual and intriguing about how he approached strength and conditioning.

Gus never openly talked about his martial arts past, and it wasn't widely accepted in the league or anywhere. But everyone knew, and he was given a lot of latitude. That said, I noticed some of the guys seemed to have different workout routines than the rest of the team. I asked what they were doing, and they mentioned Gus's martial arts past and how the workouts he gave them were the toughest things they ever done. That was all I needed to hear.

They weren't wrong.

At first it was all about stretching, strength, and cardio. But the harder I worked, the more Gus teased me with different forms and disciplines. I think he loved the fact that he couldn't push me hard enough.

"Jason, you're made of a different metal," he'd often say. After a year we really got into the martial arts end of it, and I loved it.

Looking back, mostly I was drawn to the man and the workout. The fluidity of motion, how to move people, use misdirection, evade and get inside a defense, and where to grab someone. How to get behind somebody quickly, feint one way or another—or give the appearance of moving one way when you're actually going another. How to look like you're backing up when you're actually moving in and all the subtle things you could do to redirect or control.

Mostly I was drawn to the man and the art form itself. Mostly.

But—in a big way—I was also drawn to the fact that a master of this form of martial arts could control their opponent. Control—it was also about control.

I think confidence and control go hand in hand. And control is a very good thing when the word "self" is in front of it. Self-control is evidence that the Holy Spirit is with us. It's the evidence you are free.[11] And I learned self-control with Gus. But it was not just about self-control. I was intrigued by martial arts because it was also about the ability to control another person.

For most of my life, I bought into the lie that power is defined by one's ability to control another. But maybe more to the point, I'd believed powerlessness was the inability to control another person. The whole world engages in this idea about power—even the church. Of course, Jesus revealed power in a profoundly different way. Jesus revealed that power was about sacrificial love; it was about knowing He was loved and becoming love; it was about laying one's life down for another.

But let's put a pin in that for now.

Power through controlling another is a powerfully intoxicating lie. Especially for a person who has been abused, used, or has felt powerless or helplessly controlled. This type of power gives a false sense of security. And I was desperate for security.

I had subconsciously determined I would never be a powerless person again. I would never, ever again be helpless or controlled. At the time I couldn't have articulated these last thoughts but, in hindsight, that's part of what made martial arts intriguing.

I trained with Gus for four years. I rarely talked about my martial arts training with family, friends, or teammates, but everyone knew. And I loved my reputation and how it only added to the narrative of Jason Grimsley, a dangerous man.

THE EMPATHY SWITCH

Understand, I was a fun guy. Loving and loyal, fearless and wild, always looking out for my friends and interested in everyone having a good time. I was a good teammate, on and off the field. And this went for every kind of team, including in later years my own family.

I loved a good fight and the stories that could be told about it after, but I was never looking to hurt people. I didn't want to break arms or crush knees. It was all in good fun, unless it wasn't. If I felt backed into a corner or unjustly attacked, or that a teammate or someone I loved was in danger or wronged—especially if he or she was vulnerable—an internal switch flipped. And then I became cold, calm, and dangerous. Yep, not a man to be messed with.

That switch? I treated it for many years as a savior, but ultimately it became my tormentor and my enslaver. When that switch was flipped, God help the person upon whom I placed my attention. I became emotionless, cold, and controlled—and then explosive. I moved with precision and intention to disable, subdue, and control my enemy. When the switch got flipped, I was unempathetic and unfeeling.

Though I didn't understand it then, I can tell you now what was happening.

You see, for someone who has been victimized, it's better not to feel than to feel helpless. I had put my childhood abuse and broken feelings of shame and condemnation in a box and buried that box. Throughout my life, I did everything I could to keep the box buried. But it was resurrected every time I felt vulnerable in any way. If someone slighted me or one of my teammates, or if I felt someone was trying to control me or one of my teammates—including my wife and kids—in any way, the switch was flipped. God help that person.

The fact is, I created that switch to protect myself. I couldn't show any weakness, and I refused to ever be vulnerable again. I wasn't gonna let anybody take advantage of me, embarrass me, talk down to me, or think they had the upper hand. I wasn't gonna let anybody use me, and I wasn't gonna be a victim. No matter how small the matter, in no way, shape, or form would I ever be a victim again.

I was not a man to be messed with. Full stop. End of story.

And it does end your story.

The more I fed that reputation, the more it stuck, and the more pride I took in it. But the more I fed it, the more enslaved I became to that reputation. And the more enslaved I was, the more switches that got flipped. And so, the cycle continued.

Then add ego to the scenario. I got to a point where I took pride in the fact that everybody thought I was a badass who would rip their heads off if crossed. And pride comes before a fall. That switch, the one with which empathy could be turned off, haunted me for years and tried to kill me in my 40s.

My reputation as a good teammate came from empathy, a deep place from which I sought connection, and a trait to be proud of. My reputation as a man not to be messed with was about survival, and empathy had no place there. Empathy could get you killed or taken advantage of. And I would never be taken advantage of again.

But there's nothing scarier than an unempathetic man. And there's nothing more self-damaging than being an unempathetic man. Today I have a deep empathy for that little boy named Jason Grimsley and any other person who might feel what he felt. For many years, that switch was an unhealthy coping mechanism to protect that lost little kid so he would never have to feel that way again. But I know now that way leads to an absolutely devastating loneliness.

When you spend your entire life trying to portray the image that nobody better mess with you, you find yourself alone. Or worse, you find yourself feeling alone in a room full of people who love you. You see, if you turn off empathy and feelings, you can't be vulnerable. And that cuts you off from connection, deep friendship, and the kind of trust that leads to joy and peace and fullness of life. It wasn't until I was in my late 40s and shared about the abuse with a good counselor that I began to understand the switch and how to re-engage with empathy the way Jesus lived it.

EMPATHY LIKE JESUS

Empathy is "the ability to share someone else's feelings or experiences by imagining what it would be like to be in that person's situation."[12] Jesus is the greatest expression of empathy. God didn't just imagine what it would be like to be us, He became human, too: "The Word became flesh and dwelt among us."[13]

Jesus was fully God and fully man. The act of God becoming human is the most empathetic act that's ever been done. God stepped inside our experience and our confusion, our hopes and dreams, and revealed what it looks like to be both fully human and fully one with God. Jesus showed us what it is to be confident in the love of God, and then Jesus went to a cross so we could access this same way of being human.

God went to a cross where He took sin and death to the grave. Jesus stepped inside our broken experiences and felt every one of them. He felt the helplessness of that boy Jason Grimsley, and he felt the fears of my youth. He felt the frantic shame and the reputation of a badass that I hid behind in my 20s. He felt the behavior-focused striving to be saved that marked my 30s and the desperate loneliness that haunted my 40s. He was there the day I put a gun to my head, and He felt that overwhelming sense of worthlessness.

On a cross, God was with me, He never left me, and His empathetic act of sacrificial love set me free. And I have been awakening to this love my whole life. I've written this book to tell my story so it might encourage you in your story. And I've written this chapter so you might know that wherever you are, Jesus is with you. But more than just with you, He has felt what you feel, and your salvation is discovered in saying yes to His redeeming love for you.

I still have moments when the empathy switch gets flipped, moments when I find myself traversing that lonely road. But I am learning to have empathy like Jesus. I am awakening to God's never-leaving, relentlessly redeeming love. To receiving and giving it away. And the person who has taught me this the most, who has modeled a love that never leaves, who has forgiven and stayed and challenged and walked as an expression of empathy like Jesus—well, her name is Dana.

So, let me tell you about the girl.

CHAPTER FIVE

The Girl

A love that only time can measure. Filled with the wonder of life's simple pleasures. Though simple in nature, complex in design. Each interwoven with adventures of two lives.

—For Dana

THE GIRL IN THE BLUE SAILOR SUIT

I saw her as soon as I walked in. Couldn't miss her. She lit up the room. Shimmering blonde hair, bright-eyed, and beautiful. Wearing that blue sailor outfit like she owned the whole world. She certainly owned the Clearwater, Florida, Chamber of Commerce event that I had been asked to attend as a Philly player. It was a suit and tie thing, so I was looking good too—at least, that's how she tells it.

"He was very confident." I was. I walked straight over to her, first thing. "And handsome, good-looking, and athletic, which I like." Score. "And he was very nice to me."

I was nice. But good God, she was easy to be nice to. We talked for a moment, and she introduced her mom, the woman who was hosting the event in connection with a local real estate company. I learned she was a Louisiana girl, visiting Clearwater to help her mom and stepdad run a restaurant called Fraternity House. I learned she worked with—and was close to—her brother, and that her stepdad was in the process of opening a chain of drive thru restaurants up and down the east coast called Checkers. She learned that I loved their hot dogs, fries, and burgers. She also learned that I was a Texas boy and heard a little about how I came to play pro ball. We left the event, picked up friends, and met up at a club.

She was radiant and fun. But the more we talked, the more I realized there was a problem. You see, she was a keeper, what you call a long-term project. The kind of girl you brought home to meet Mom. I was a Major League baseball player in my prime. Another way to say it: I was the cliché, the walking ego, a Don Juan, a player. I was the kind of guy who was looking to hook up. Yeah, an idiot. This was the early 90s, when dating and monogamy were culturally equated to a prison sentence and Hollywood told us that real men slept with lots of women. And I'd bought stock in that lie.

Around 1:30 a.m., Dana invited me and my buddies to continue the fun by joining her and her friends for breakfast. But I said, "Nah, I gotta get home; gotta wake up pretty early to work out." She nodded, smiled dazzlingly, wrote down her number on a piece of paper, put it in my wallet, and then went to hang with her friends.

"She's amazing," I thought as I watched her go. Then I joined my buddies with the girls I knew weren't long term. Shortly after, I stood outside the club waiting for my truck. Dana walked out with her friends, looked at me, saw the girl at my side, smiled playfully and said, "You gotta get up early? I see."

Damn. She caught me. I imagined that would be the last time I saw her. But a few weeks later after a practice, I walked out to my truck to find a note under the windshield wiper: "Hi, it's Dana. My cousin is in town, and we're going out. Give me a call." After hearing about me, Dana's cousin had suggested that Dana shouldn't wait for me to call her. They drove to the Phillies' Spring Training stadium, talked the security guy into letting them into the players' parking lot, found a truck with Texas plates, figured correctly that I was the kind of fella who drove a truck, and left a note—along with Dana's number.

I remembered that smile and called. It was a hell of a first date. We even slept together. And she rolls her eyes every time I tell the story that way, 'cause we didn't actually sleep together. Here is what actually happened:

"Why didn't you call me?" she asked playfully.

"I lost your number." I actually thought I had.

She studied me a moment, a smile on the corner of her lips. "Oh yeah?" Then she put out her hand and said, "Let me see your wallet." She was so self-confident that I obeyed without thinking. She opened the wallet, pulled out the piece of paper with her number on it, and held it up. "This number?" she asked, amusement in her eyes. "Is this the number you lost?"

Damn. She caught me. Again. "She is amazing," I thought. But I said, "Oh, I thought I'd lost it." I lied, and both of us knew it.

"Uh huh," she responded, unimpressed.

Dana's mom leased luxury furnished condos, and we ended up hanging out in one of the unrented units where we talked and laughed and dreamed the whole night. At one point, we even fell asleep, and that's where the joke comes from. But there was no fooling around. I really liked her, and she wasn't that kind of girl. Like I said, she was the kind you took home to Mom. And that's exactly what I told her. Well, not exactly, but close. By the end of that night, I knew she was the one.

"I'm gonna marry you," I said.

"Yeah, that's not gonna work," she responded.

"No, I'm serious. I'm gonna marry you. I even know what kind of wedding we're gonna have. It's gonna be black-and-white themed, and the flowers will be lilies."

She looked at me and smiled as if to say, "Yeah, we'll see." But she didn't respond.

The night became morning and the date ended. We saw each other every day for about a month. Then I went back to baseball, and she went back to Louisiana. We talked a lot at first. She was incredible, but as the weeks passed, I stopped calling her—and not because I didn't like her. When I thought about my future, I found myself thinking about her. But remember, I'd bought stock in my ego. I was a pro ball player in his prime, a real man who wouldn't be tied down to one woman (and all that bullshit).

It would take a wake-up call to get out of my own way. And it came weeks later in the form of a breakup letter from Dana—a letter that informed me she absolutely loved spending time hanging out but didn't think we were right for each other and that the long-distance thing wasn't working. I told her I never received it.

The letter revealed to me how I felt: I didn't want to lose this girl. As soon as I read it, I called her, and I never stopped. When the season ended, I drove to Louisiana to see her almost weekly.

Revelation: with each passing day I knew one thing—I wanted to be with Dana.

After that night, Dana was all I could think about. She was everything. She was beautiful, smart, and knew how to have fun. She loved to laugh and was witty. She was grounded, good, and kind. Did I mention hot? Yeah, that too. And she was confident. But it wasn't conceited—she was simply sure, strong. She knew what she wanted in life and wasn't willing to compromise.

But she was also vulnerable. She let me protect her and play the man. And I wanted to be the man, her man. I wanted to provide for and look after her. Though I couldn't have articulated it when I first met her, she was the steady to my full-throttle life, the calm to my storm. Don't get me wrong, Dana can storm. She isn't weak; she's fearless and can release holy hell if it's needed. You especially don't want to come between her and her kids. But she isn't cruel; she is steady and unmoving. She has always been my rock.

And above all, she was for me. Somehow, she knew me—the real me—even when I acted the fool. Even when my ego ruled the day, she could see past it to who I truly am and love me. To this day, even though I've put her through hell at times, she sees the man God designed, the man who loves her and our kids and wants to be all God has called him to be. She's always had my back and that's everything to a guy like me.

I don't know God's role in these things. I have friends who were Christians before they met their spouses, and they speak to God's influence in their decision. But at the time, I wasn't really thinking about God or talking to Him. That said, you couldn't convince me that Dana wasn't God's perfect plan. People these days talk about "the one" and how that's not really a thing. Well, I can't speak for others, but Dana is the one for me, no doubt about it.

In October 1990, we were on the phone, and I asked, "What would you say if I asked you to marry me?"

"I guess I'd say, yes," she responded.

The conversation moved on and eventually we hung up. As soon as I put the phone down, I went to my truck and drove to Coats Jewelers and bought a ring. Then, I drove to her home in Louisiana, just outside of New Orleans. She was at work, but her stepmom, Phyllis, was home.

I walked in with ring in my pocket. Phyllis excitedly helped me set everything up. I put the ring on Rookie, a big white teddy bear I'd bought for her months earlier, placed it in her room, and hid just up the stairs until Dana returned from work. Usually, Dana went straight to her room to change. Not this time. I hid and listened to her play with the dogs, talk with Phyllis is and mess around for about fifteen minutes; I was so excited, it felt like hours.

Finally, she went into her room, and I heard her scream, "Where is he?"

She came running out to find me on one knee. "Will you marry me?" I asked.

The bold girl who knew what she wanted, who'd tracked me down to remind me to call her, who'd sent me a break-up letter that woke me up to my love for her, smiled like the rising sun and said, "Yes."

So, on Feb 7, 1991—eleven months after we met—we were married. It was a black-and-white themed affair, with lilies.

BATSHIT CRAZY

It was a road game, and I was sharing a room with my friend Jerry Dipoto. Jerry is the GM for the Seattle Mariners now, but back then he was a teammate with the Cleveland Indians. We went out after the game and got a few beers; Jerry decided to leave early. He took the only hotel room key with him.

I got back to the hotel about 2:30 a.m. to a locked door. I banged on the front door for half an hour, but nobody was there. Then I worked my way around the building, banging on side doors. Again, nobody answered.

Around 3:15 a.m. I realized that if I didn't figure out how to get in the room, I was gonna have to sleep on the street. Then I got an idea. I knew our room number was 712, the 7th floor. I knew the rooms with even numbers were on one side of the building and odds were on the other. And each room had outdoor balconies with wrought iron railings.

The solution was simple. I counted up seven floors, over twelve, determined what room was mine, took a deep breath, jumped up, grabbed the bottom of the first-floor balcony, pulled myself up, and climbed over. Then I did it again. One balcony after another, I climbed until I'd counted to seven. I jumped down off the railing onto the balcony with a sense of satisfaction and relief, thinking, "That was kinda crazy."

I checked the sliding glass door. It was unlocked. Then a thought hit me: what if I had miscalculated? So, I gently and quietly slide the door open. It was dark inside, so I stood just behind the curtain and let my eyes adjust. Then, slowly, I parted the curtains. This was not my room!

My newly adjusted eyes saw a sleeping man and woman in one bed, a kid in the other. "Oh shit," I thought with nervous humor as I slowly backed out of the room and ever so gently closed the sliding door. Confused, I went to the railing, looked down and counted: one, two, three, four, five, six, seven, eight. "Oh shit," I thought again. I hadn't considered the first floor and had climbed one too many. I was on the eighth floor.

"Now what?" I wondered, knowing and dreading the answer.

The thing about climbing is that going up is way easier than going down. You can see what you're grabbing. Going down? Well, if my heart beat a little faster on the way up, it raged as I climbed over the railing of the eight-floor balcony.

"This is crazy. Batshit crazy," I thought as I grabbed hold of the spindles, slid down to the bottom, extended my arms and hung my

6'3" body until the tip of my big toe—the one I still had on my right foot—brushed the top of the seventh-floor balcony rail.

Then, letting go of the rail with one hand, I reached under and leveraged the ceiling of the 7th floor, my weight supported fully, landing on the 7th floor railing. Balance, lean, and a leap. I landed on the balcony floor with the adrenaline flowing. I stood there for a minute and caught my breath. Then, praying to a God I didn't yet know that this was in fact my room, I opened the unlocked sliding glass door to the reassuringly familiar sounds of my teammates Jerry Dipoto and Tommy Kramer playing video games. I grinned. Then, adding to my fearless reputation, I split the curtains and walked in as if I'd used the front door.

Both guys jumped and Jerry yelled, "What the hell!"

I shrugged. "You took the key."

He stared at me, then ran past and out onto the balcony, looked down, then looked back at me with shock. "What's wrong with you?" If I had a dollar. . .

After I'd proposed, I called Dana's mom, stepdad, other stepdad, and dad to ask permission to marry their daughter. Or at least, to respectfully honor the tradition. Dana's mom and stepdad hadn't yet heard the story about climbing balconies, but they'd met me and knew I was a little … extra. Dana's stepdad actually hung up the phone. He wasn't too keen on Dana marrying a pro athlete.

"You sure you want to marry a ballplayer?" he asked Dana. "That life is hard. You're constantly moving, everything is up in the air, and they are crazy."

I had already asked her the same question before we walked the aisle. With more emphasis on crazy, I said, "You sure you want to do this? You know I'm batshit crazy."

But we were young and invincible, as was our love. Life was full of possibility, travel, and the kinds of friendships that are lifelong. Dana couldn't be dissuaded by balcony climbs or all the other bullshit because she knew what she wanted: to marry me and have babies.

Plus, my batshit crazy was as attractive to her as her calm steady was to me. Well, maybe not quite as much. She may have reminded Jerry once or twice to make sure I had my own room key before we left for a road game. And it was easy for her to remind Jerry because we ended up sharing an apartment with him and his new bride, Tamie, that first year of marriage during spring training.

They were—and still are—some of those lifelong friends. We had a lot of fun with them. Dana and Tamie got along well as they both were pretty focused on the same thing: trying to get pregnant. So, while I chased my dream of pro ball, Dana chased her dream by doing that whole temperature thing. It's some temperature-taking method to track ovulation so you know when's the best day to get pregnant.

I'd come home from a road game or practice and Dana would say, "Okay, it's time to take a nap." Which was code for, "Let's make a baby." But it wasn't a secret code because it was the same one Jerry and Tamie used. Dana and Tamie ended up getting pregnant on the same day.

BABIES

Nothing expands your heart and your capacity to love like becoming a parent. Hunter came first. Dana was in labor for a few hours. I remember I was pretty damn excited. I also remember the doc being one hell of a good guy. He was a hunter, so we had much to talk about during the labor. Dana said we talked duck hunting the whole time she was pushing; she says it as though it was a bad thing, but I remember it differently.

Hunter was stunning. I loved him with my whole heart. And no, he wasn't named during labor; we'd decided on Hunter before he came. Sixteen months later, we were back in the hospital, same doctor, less talk about hunting. But he echoed my high school coach, Rick Lynch's, question about whether we would stick with a theme: "What's this one going to be called, Fisher?" We went with John and called him John-John for most of his childhood. He was beautiful, and my heart expanded.

And that's the wild thing about love—it's measureless. The moment you think you have its measure—the moment you think you couldn't love more—your heart grows. This has been my discovery about God's love as well. The moment I think I've understood just how much He loves me, I discover to my wonder that there is no end to His love for me. Or for you.

It's like those verses in Ephesians:

> And I pray that you, being rooted and established in love, may have power, together with all the Lord's holy people, to grasp how wide and long and high and deep is the love of Christ, and to know this love that surpasses knowledge—that you may be filled to the measure of all the fullness of God. Now to him who is able to do immeasurably more than all we ask or imagine, according to his power that is at work within us.[14]

The apostle Paul essentially describes God's love as wide, long, high, and deep, and then invites the reader to be filled to the measure of this love. Then the next verse blows my mind by describing love as "immeasurably more than all we ask or imagine."

I didn't think I could love anyone the way I loved Dana, and then Hunter came along, and I had the same thought about him. Then

John-John revealed once again that love is wide, and long, and high, and deep, and beyond my ability to measure. And then, three years later, we had Rayne. She was stunning, beautiful beyond imagining. My girl. My heart. My joy. And once again, my heart expanded as measureless love invaded.

Rayne was named after a town close to Lafayette, and Dana always loved the name. Rayne has finally come around to it.

With each child, I discovered this greater reality of why I'm on earth: to love my kids, to be their dad, to be there for them in every way I can, and to grow more available as I grow surer in love. You feel this the moment your child is born. It's a lifetime of failing and asking forgiveness and growing in love to live it out. As I mentioned, family is the long game.

There is nothing more transformative than loving another person selflessly.

And in those early years while God walked beside me but I didn't know it, I tasted of His love through my love for Dana and when I held each of my children in my arms. I have since come to understand that God is love, so to begin to know Him is to simply stop and recognize love when you experience it.

It can happen while in conversation with a friend, or in parenting, or while reading a book. But God is love, so when we know or feel that self-giving love for one another, that is God speaking to and through us. And the more we practice recognizing this, the more fluent we become in how God acts and speaks. I think this is why we know God is real when we finally say yes to Him. We are overwhelmed by forgiveness, mercy, grace, and all expressions of His love. I also think we have all experienced love in our lives and salvation is simply about the day we recognize and surrender everything to the Author of love.

For me, marrying Dana and then having kids was the most powerful way I experienced love. In hindsight, I can see how God was walking beside me in those early days, revealing Himself to me, even when I didn't know Him. Even when my own brokenness and insecurities kept getting in the way.

And hindsight is the point. Because love is a two-way street. First John 4:19 says, "We love because God first loved us." To love someone well is to make yourself vulnerable. I didn't do vulnerable well back then. Hell, I am still learning in that area. But back then, when I first become a husband and father and while I was tasting of God's love through my relationship with Dana and my kids, I was still hiding past hurt and shame and protecting myself behind a growing ego—behind the reputation of a man not to be messed with.

So, while I was experiencing the most amazing things—a family and a baseball career—I was also experiencing fear and shame. From a distance, we looked like the perfect family. And so much of what we had *was* perfect, but perception and reality aren't always the same thing. Context is everything.

PERCEPTION AND CONTEXT

Sometimes you can watch something take place, even be a part of the whole experience, and still miss the context needed to understand the whole story.

For instance, in 1990 I was with the Phillies, and we were in LA playing the Dodgers. The Dodgers were hitting. And there was a play at third base; it was a bang-bang play. It was close and the umpire called the runner out. Well, out of the dugout came the late great, one and only, Tommy Lasorda, the GM of the Dodgers. I'd say he sprinted out, but Tommy didn't sprint, he waddled.

And Tommy was hot. He got up to the umpire and he was screaming, hollering, poking his fist, kicking dirt, and throwing his hands up. He was looking at the crowd and getting them riled up. Then he turned around, poked the umpire in the chest, threw dirt on him, waddled over to the third base, picked the base up, pointed at the base, put it back in the dirt, and kicked dirt on it. He pointed at the umpire again, hollering the whole time, and then he turned around and waddled back to his dugout.

I was watching from the bench and the whole time I—along with everyone in the stadium—was waiting for the umpire to throw Tommy out of the game. But the ump just stood there taking it until Tommy was spent, and then the game went on like it hadn't happened. Everyone on the bench, in the stadium. and watching around the world was wondering, "What in the world just happened?"

I didn't have to wait long to get context. The next day at the ballpark, a teammate came up and said, "Jason, you're not gonna believe this. Last night, after the game, I asked the ump why he didn't throw Lasorda out."

"What'd he say?" I asked.

He said, "How am I going to throw a guy out when all he's doing is screaming, 'That is the best call I've ever seen in my life! I can't believe you got it right! It was that close on this bag, and you got the call right in front all these people! It's amazing, the best damn call I've ever seen! Right here! On this base! In front of all these people!'?" Then he turned around and walked off."

Perception and reality aren't always the same thing. Context is everything.

Those early years with Dana and our growing family were amazing. I was young and still had hair; I was good looking, chasing my dream, and ready to take on the world with my beautiful, bright, hopeful, and confident girl. Hell, there was no room I wanted to be in that didn't have Dana in it. And with each child, the future became even brighter. That was the truth. Even when I screwed the whole thing up; even when I lost my way. But also, context is everything.

This is the second stanza of a poem I wrote Dana a few years ago.

> *Two lives that have weathered days full of storms.*
> *Also, times of joy—neither one the norm.*
> *To live life as it comes, facing the future hand in hand.*
> *The hardship of loss, in our walk along the sand.*

This was written as a love letter to my girl, a poem to recognize how two lives have weathered difficult storms; a journaling that reveals how our hopeful perceptions often clashed violently with our context. Those early days, we were living the dream. But again, context is everything.

Our context included that Dana had grown up with a mom who had been married several times. She had several stepdads along the way. She knew she was loved, but she had lived through the insecurity of broken family. When she married me, she was looking for a person who could protect her and provide a safe home to raise a family. Our context also included my childhood, the ego and reputation I'd developed to protect that little boy, and my life-and-death need to defend everyone I loved. That context was a part of our sincere love for one another. We were a good fit, a good match, and our love for each other was honest, but there were cracks in the foundation, mostly on my end.

You see, Dana was an open book. She was solid, and I loved her for it, and I needed her for it. I think her steadiness came from her faith. It was a young faith when we first married, but no less sincere. Dana understood God as Love. Even when she wrestled with feelings of worthlessness, she knew the answer and solution to that ache was somehow discovered in God's love.

That's a really good place to look for the answers; in fact, it's the only place. But that's not where I looked. I wasn't an open book. I wasn't vulnerable. I hid my insecurities and fears behind my ever-growing reputation. Over the years, as the context of my brokenness began to kick perception in the teeth, Dana leaned ever more into her faith in a God who loves, a God who saves, a God who redeems, and a God who restores. Meanwhile, I dove deeper into the god of my ego.

The fact is, it's because of the grace of God that we are together today. And for many years, the grace of God in my life went by the name Dana. Dana is part of God's best idea for my life, a rock. I am not calling her Savior; I am simply stating that her faith in our Savior is the reason I'm here today writing this book and the reason our family is still a family.

I knew she was the girl for me the day I proposed, and I know it a million times more today. The best thing I ever did was marry the bold girl who knew what she wanted. The girl who'd tracked me down to remind me to call her, the girl who'd sent me a breakup letter that woke me up to my love for her, and the girl who has increasingly modeled God's faithful love. And I am forever in love.

> *There is no secret spell or mysterious way;*
> *It is loving each other day after day.*

CHAPTER SIX

The Truth About Control

JOE BICK

I met my agent, Joe Bick, in 1986. I hired him on the spot, and he has been stuck with me ever since. Joe is a good man; he's always had my back, not just as my agent but as a friend. He's made a great impact on many baseball players' lives. He's old school—a true advocate for his players in the game and in life. And Joe is a great storyteller. If you were to call him about baseball, he could tell some good tales, and if you called to ask him about me, it's no different.

In a recent conversation with a friend, I heard the story from Joe's perspective:

> I signed Jason during his first Spring Training in Clearwater, Florida. He was in the Minor League camp for the Phillies; he was eighteen years old. I don't know what Jason's spin rates were, but they were off the charts. Nobody measured that kind of thing back then. Jason was such a likable guy—and a stubborn knot head!

I met his mom and dad and got close with them. I love his dad, Johnny. He is such a nice guy; as good-natured as anybody I've ever met. I asked him once where Jason got his temper because it couldn't have been from him. He said, "Oh, he must have gotten it from his mother."

Anyway, I learned right away that Jason had a strong sense of right and wrong and a high value for his teammates, friends, and his new agent. And he wouldn't back down from anybody.

I was in Florida, just met and signed Jason two days earlier, and I told him and another of my players with the Phillies—a pitcher named Scott Service—that I was going to the Phillies night game because I had a player on the other team that was playing. The game was in Jack Russell Stadium, an old beat-up stadium.

Anyway, they said, "We're going to the game too. You can just sit with us."

"You sure?" I asked. I knew all the Minor League guys had to go to the games, and they would all sit together on a couple of sets of bleachers right beside the bullpen.

"Am I allowed to sit down there with you guys?" I asked.

"Yeah, you're allowed; it's not a problem."

So, I met them at the game and was sitting with them and about twenty-five other Minor League Philly players on the bleachers, when Tony Segal walked up. Tony was a Minor League director at the time, a guy who ended up being a baseball executive for many years. But I hadn't met Tony yet.

"Can I ask who you are?" Tony said.

"Joe Bick. I'm an agent. Scott and Jason are both clients of mine."

Tony said, "Well, this section is for our players only. You're not going to be able to sit down here during the game."

I apologized, "No problem. I'm happy to move. I wasn't trying to sneak in anywhere. The guys thought it was okay if I if I sat down here with them."

So, I stood up to leave, but before I could fully rise, Grimsley, who was sitting beside me, grabbed the back of my pant leg and sat me back down. Then he looked at Tony and said, "We invited him to sit down here, and he ain't going anywhere."

I looked at Jason thinking, "What are you doing?" Then I said to Tony, "No, no, no. I'm happy to move if I'm not supposed to be here."

But for the next fifteen minutes Jason—an eighteen-year-old kid in Spring Training for the first time—went nose-to-nose arguing with Tony Segal. I left and watched the whole thing from further up the stands. When it was over Jason came up to where I was sitting.

"Why in God's name would you do that?" I said. "You're a new guy down here. You don't need to be getting into fights with Tony Segal. He's a guy you need to have on your side." And that was the beginning. I should've known right then!

For the next twenty-two years, Jason and I talked two to three times a week, and we still talk regularly. Jason became closer than a friend. I'm seventy years old, but he is the brother I never had. He's so different from me personality-wise and upbringing-wise. But I hope Jason Grimsley lays me in my grave one day.

After finishing, Joe chokes up and manages to say, "Yeah, I love Jason."

Hearing Joe's story brings tears to my eyes. Man, I could write a whole book on all the times Joe saved me. All the times I called him, and he went to work; all the times I made his job harder. And though he'd never say it—all the times he had my back. Joe was not just my agent. I feel the same way: Joe is like a brother to me, and I love him.

He's been with me through it all, including the early days when I wrestled just to make it. He's been with me through the greatest highs and the darkest lows. I am thankful for Joe, and I know I made him work his ass off. I can't tell you how many times he answered the phone only to hear me tell him about how I went toe-to-toe with my pitching coach, the manager—hell, even league executives. I don't know how many times Joe heard me say, "I'm headed home."

I'LL DIG A FRICKIN DITCH...

In such a highly competitive industry, I knew very early on that I was just a commodity. I knew I was only on a team as long as I could throw a baseball. And I knew most of the league didn't value me like I valued myself. But I never thought about it in terms of dollars and cents. I thought about it in terms of respect. I loved to play baseball, but if I couldn't play, or felt disrespected along the way? Well, I always figured I could dig a ditch. This motivation meant I was free to chase down the dream. It also meant I was free to tell those who didn't respect me to go screw themselves, which I did on more than one occasion.

The first time was when I was eighteen. The director of the Minor Leagues was gonna send me somewhere I didn't think I deserved go. "Go fuck yourself," I said. Dana and I had been married less than a year when I got traded to the Astros. So, we moved to Tucson, Arizona, where I played out that season on their Triple-A ball club. I had a so-so year in the Pacific Coast League.

Then, in '93, I went to Spring Training with the Astros. I had a ridiculous Spring Training: four wins and a save in pre-season. It was the kind of Spring Training that gets you called up with a payday of $100,000. But just before the season kicked off, literally as we were on the bus to Houston for the first game, Fred Nelson, the Director of the Minor Leagues, and Bob Watson, the GM, pulled me off the bus and into the office with an ultimatum: "Jason, we want a pitcher by the name of Brian Williams—one of the guys we drafted high, one of our guys—to be the starter. So, we're gonna send you to Triple-A with the $100,000, as we don't think anyone else would pay that."

Essentially, I'd played good enough to start on most teams within the League, but instead of releasing me so I could potentially find a roster spot somewhere else, they'd waited till the last moment to try and stash me on their Triple-A team as an insurance policy if Brian Williams didn't do anything. And they'd hoped—no, more, they'd expected—I'd take the money and play for their Triple-A team.

But I didn't just play for money. I wanted respect, and there's nothing I hate more than being used. I didn't take too kindly to their news. "Fred, I want you to have them take my truck off the transport freightliner. I'm grabbing my suitcase and heading home."

Both Fred and Bob took turns telling me, "You can't do this. It's the last day of Spring Training—nobody's gonna pick you up."

But I was done. "Boys, I'll dig a frickin ditch before I ever play for you guys. Get my truck off the freightliner. I'm going to the house."

"Jason, you need to think about this."

"I don't need to think about shit. I will not play baseball for you."

I called Joe while I waited for my truck. Then on the way home, I called Dana on my new car phone. In our young marriage, it wasn't the first time she'd gotten the call about a change in my status, just the next in what would be many more. But it was the first time she'd heard about how I'd told off the brass.

"I'm headed home," I told her, and she said, "Okay."

But before I made it home, my new car phone rang. It was Joe, "The Indians called; they want you in Charlotte, North Carolina."

"I'll be there." So, Dana and I went to Charlotte, North Carolina, where I played with my favorite manager of all time, Charlie Manual. Great guy—a character from Wheeling, West Virginia.

CHARLIE MANUAL

Charlie called me "Rattler" because as he put it, "Son, you're as mean as a rattlesnake." Where I was just a commodity to the Astros, I was a person to Charlie. There was a lot of God in how Charlie communicated to me. Not sure Charlie would see it that way. He had a mouth like a sailor, but I felt respected by Charlie. And respect is a simple way to value someone. Charlie saw me, truly. He wasn't thrown off by my ego; he saw past all the bravado and insecurity. And even more, he believed in me.

I remember the first game I pitched. We were playing Columbus, the Yankees' Triple-A team, and a guy hit it off me—I'm talking a moonshot. And all I hear from the dugout is Charlie Manual yelling with his West Virginia drawl, "Oh no, not my man Grims, get back fence."

I came in after the inning and Charlie laughed good naturedly, "Hoo-oo, son, he got that one, didn't he?" That was Charlie. I love the guy. He rolled with the punches, took everything in stride, and had your back. And I mean, he truly had my back.

I remember we had a day game in Virginia Beach. After the game, some of the players and I went out to a restaurant. I had a beer and walked out of the restaurant with the beer in my hand after dinner. I finished it and then put it in the trash can. Immediately, a police officer on a bicycle came up and threatened to give me a ticket. Apparently, it was an open container issue or something. But he was just being a disrespectful ass. Well, I didn't like it too much.

First, he was on a bicycle. That pissed me off.

Second, he was wearing shorts. That pissed me off.

Third, considering I was already pissed off, I decided I didn't like his red hair. Now, I've got nothing against redheads, but this one was a smart ass.

"You really gonna give me a ticket?" I asked as he handed me a ticket.

"Yeah!" he said, flexing his bicycle-riding, shorts-wearing, red-headed authority.

Well, I didn't like it, so I waded up the ticket and threw it at him.

That did it. Thank God I didn't swing at him, but I didn't make it easy. And he wasn't gentle. And when his buddies arrived, they jumped on me, got the handcuffs on me, and beat the shit out of me. Then I was put in the back of a paddy wagon, and that's when my teammates decided I was on my own. They didn't go get Charlie. Didn't even tell Charlie.

So there I was sitting in the Virginia Beach jail with knots on my head, one eye bloodied closed, bruises on my back, blood coming out of my ear, and wrists cut because the handcuffs had been so tight. At about midnight they pulled me in front of the judge.

He gave one look at me, then asked, "What's the arrest for? What the hell did he do?"

"Littering," the cop said.

The judge was immediately irate. Hell, I've never seen a scolding quite like the one he gave, and I was a professional ball player for twenty years. He unloaded on the guys. He *mother "f'ed"* them up and down. Then he turned his attention to me, "Son, if they hadn't processed you, I'd turn your ass loose, but you're in the system. Who can you call?"

The chastised cop uncuffed me and took me into the judge's office so I could use his phone. I called Charlie in his hotel room.

He answered, and it was clear I'd woken him. *"Uh, uh, uh ... he—he—hello?"*

"Charlie, it's Grims."

"What the heck all three son? What time is it?"

"It's midnight."

"What the fuck you are calling me for?"

"Charlie, I'm in a little bit a trouble. I'm in jail."

"Oh, fuck Grims. Who'd you kill?"

"Nobody Charlie! Could you come get me?"

"Yeah, yeah. I'll be right there."

While he and Dyer Miller, my pitching coach, got in their maroon Cadillac rental car and drove down to Virginia Beach to bail me out, the judge and I sat in his office and talked baseball. He was a good fella. Charlie and Dyer bailed me out.

When we got in the car Charlie asked, "Grims, do you know that judge?"

"No, sir."

"Well, that son-a-bitch sure does like you."

Charlie never told the Indians, never told anybody in the front office. It was never in the papers—nothing. And I am thankful for how he handled it. He could have quit on me, thought of me as too much trouble. I mean, it's not like it was the first time I'd caused trouble.

Let's rewind a little bit. I'd been in Charlotte for only two weeks, and we were on a road trip to Columbus, Ohio. In the first three innings, I punched out six guys: strike outs. They didn't get a ball out of the infield. Then, in the fourth inning, suddenly I couldn't strike out anyone. They were all hitting bullets. Four runs later, I got pulled.

I wasn't happy, and I was running hot. Back then, that's how I played. I wore my emotions on my sleeve; I ran hot and cold, and I took it all personally. You don't last long when you play that way, but I would learn.

Anyway, I had been on fire and then it all went to hell in a hand basket, and I was furious. So, my demeanor as I entered the dugout was south of friendly. I hit the water fountain and knocked the cooler over. And that's when my new pitching coach, Dyer Miller, grabbed me and turned me around, saying, "Hey! We don't do that shit here!" And I hit him. Straight up. He went down hard. It gets worse, too— they had to pull me off him.

Charlie came in from the field yelling, "What the heck?"

I grabbed my glove and left the dugout. I went to the club house,

took a shower, packed my bags, and called Dana. "Honey, I'm probably coming home." I said for the second time in weeks.

"What happened?" she asked.

"I hit my pitching coach."

"What is wrong with you?"

Cha-ching.

When the game was over, Charlie walked in. "Hey, Grims, I need
to see you in my office." I went in and sat down. Dyer came in and
sat next to me.

Charlie looked at me. "What the heck, son? What are you doing?"

"Look, you can scream at me and berate me all you want. But do
not touch me. I'm a grown ass man—nobody's gonna touch me like
that!"

Looking back on that moment, I can hear the little boy in me
screaming at the top of his lungs, "Nobody's gonna touch me like
that!" But at the time, I didn't have a clue about the deeper, unat-
tended wounds that were growing like a cancer within me, and if I
didn't know what was going on, there's no way Dyer or Charlie could
have understood.

But, because of who Charlie was, because he could see the person
behind the façade, and because he valued everyone, he created a culture where he could deal with people's shit in a way that empowered
reconciliation. There's a lot to pull from that last sentence.

Reconciliation—"a situation in which two people or groups of
people become friendly again after they have argued"[15]—is maybe
one of the most God-like qualities a person could have. So, while I
don't know much about Charlie's thoughts about God, he sure seemed
to know something about how to connect people with one another.

"Nobody's gonna touch me like that," hung in the air.

And to his credit, Dyer said, "Ah hell, Charlie, I shouldn't have done that."

Charlie looked at me and said, "Well, Grims, you know I gotta do something."

"I understand, Charlie." I expected he'd suspend me.

"Tell you what, you gotta buy Dyer dinner tomorrow night."

I was glad to do it and deeply grateful for Charlie's generosity. Because, the fact was, I didn't hold anything against Dyer. Hell, I liked Dyer. Still do. Charlie understood respect and knew he'd get it back when it was given. Kind of like my elementary teacher, Mr. McClin. Sometimes I'd act out, and when I did, he'd grab the paddle ('cause they still used paddles back then) and say, "Jason, let's go."

We'd walk together out of the classroom into the hallway. He'd close the door, he'd note my behavior, I'd apologize, and then he'd slap his paddle on the bottom of his shoe before instructing me to act chastised before we went back into class. Like Mr. McClin, Charlie knew how to handle me; how to see the man I wanted to be, the man I could become. And he liked me.

After I left Cleveland and I'd run into him, he'd say, "God dang it, Rattler—good to see you!" And I knew he meant it.

A BALLPLAYER'S WIFE

"I knew what kind of man he was; he wouldn't be taken advantage of. So, you never knew what was gonna happen, day to day. In many ways it was good, because he was very protective and wasn't going to take anything from anybody. He truly would rather dig a ditch than feel taken advantage of."

Those are Dana's words when asked to describe that season of our lives and what it was like being a baseball player's wife. Being a ballplayer's wife is tough. Especially when the guy you're married to is just a moment away from being traded or shipped off to a farm team. And especially when you don't understand where that deep-driving, life-impacting fear of being taken advantage of comes from. I never told Dana about my childhood. I buried it deep and not even Dana could be trusted with the information. But she felt it, even if she couldn't understand it.

"Trust is a miserable thing to want." That's how Dana once described the disconnect that grew between us. Those words are painfully true and something both of us felt. Dana found some connection with other players' wives. They sat together during games and would get together during the week, but where she found the best community was in her weekly Bible studies.

Every team has a chaplain and usually the chaplain's wife would lead Bible studies for the wives. For Dana, this was a good place to connect in deeper ways with those on a similar journey; a safe place to talk about being a ballplayer's wife and about parenting. And it was where she began to grow in her faith. She began to dive into Scripture. She read books on relationships and wholeness, forgiveness, and trust.

There are a lot of Christians in baseball who are good and honorable people—and I respected them. So, I was happy Dana seemed to find some connection there, but I didn't want anything to do with them. To me, Christians were weak, and weakness screwed with my reputation. To say it another way, weakness wasn't something I could afford.

I listened as Dana shared what she learned about God, and it was good. But when we talked, I mostly just felt like a sinner. It wasn't that Dana talked a lot about sin; it was that her pursuit of righteousness in her own life highlighted my lack thereof. It's called conviction. It's a good thing, but it's a journey and an uncomfortable one.

For years I resisted, and in many ways, we became disconnected. It wasn't that we didn't love each other. That was never a question. And it wasn't that we didn't experience profound moments of joy and connection and adventure. We did, but the more she dove into her faith, the more pressure I felt to convince her I was a good guy. The problem is, I wasn't always a good guy. I was missing the mark and I knew it. So did Dana—and that created a growing loneliness in both of us. We loved one another but each felt a deep loneliness.

Dana pursued her faith: prayer meetings, church services, Bible studies, and books on marriage and family. But because of how often we moved and her own insecurities, she never really connected deeply enough with a group or person to share her concerns about how she felt disconnected and lonely or how, later in my career, she even began to wonder if I was cheating on her.

She'd tell you now that she should have been more open, but she'd also tell you that it likely wouldn't have mattered as most of the wives were in the same position. They didn't have their husbands with them, were away from families, felt alone, and craved support.

As far as stability was concerned, one good decision we made after kids was to make home base in Louisiana. It provided consistency for Dana and the kids, which was good because the next several years were inconsistent to the point that I thought about quitting.

READY TO QUIT

In '93 I got called up and moved from Charlotte to Cleveland, where I ended up playing with the Indians in the Major Leagues through '95. They put me in the bullpen at the beginning of the season as a relief pitcher. I'd never pitched from the bullpen.

The bullpen is an area on the side of the playing field where relief pitchers warm up to come in the game later. I'll write more about it later, but at this point I'd always been a starter and had never really pitched out of the bullpen. I didn't know how to approach this new role, and Cleveland didn't have a plan to help me. They buried me there, never used me, and then sent me down.

In '96, two days into spring training, I got traded from Cleveland to the California Angels. I spent the year in the Major Leagues with them. Then, in '97, I went to Spring Training in Detroit, then got released and picked up by the Minnesota Twins. It was a miserable year with a team that had no real value for me or plan for my role with them. I'd start one game, then I'd be inactive the next, then I was relief pitching—throwing out of the bullpen for a game or two—then I was back to inactive, and around we'd go.

I grew so tired of the inconsistent nature of that team and the lack of respect, and I had grown tired of the years of bouncing around. After being made inactive again, I went to the manager's office and said, "I'm done. You can either trade me, or I'm headed to the house."

They obliged and traded me. A few days later, I was in Omaha, Nebraska, with Kansas City's Triple-A team. I finished off the season there. And by the end of it, I was exhausted and disillusioned with the whole thing. I never felt more like a commodity than that year. I was of no value to Detroit, Minnesota, or Kansas City. I came home with a bad taste in my mouth, and for the first time, serious questions about my future in baseball. I had yet to get a decent contract with a team that would commit. And while money was never the main point when it came to playing ball, I had a growing family and responsibilities.

That winter, with what little money we had, I purchased a fiberglass company that did boat repairs and built stairs. It was doing okay, and I thought about just diving into that business. It wasn't something that intrigued me, but I was so demoralized that I didn't know if I could go back to ball.

I told Dana, "I'm tired. Tired of dragging you guys around, tired of failing on a grand scale, tired of not being valued. Hell, there are players getting deals that aren't as good as I am." It was a complaint she had heard a hundred times. And it was true—I wasn't valued up to my abilities. And it pissed me off. I was angry all the time. That was part of the problem—and further—I knew it. I knew one of the reasons I had not stuck with a team and had not gotten the contract was my mental state of being.

Joe described this season of my career this way:

> There were some bumps in the road. Part of it was his frustration with himself, and part of it was his combativeness. He certainly had run-ins along the way with coaches, and there were some fracases. He was stubborn and frustrated and played that way.
>
> He was the kind of guy that, however many innings he pitched, he was going to give up a lot fewer hits than the innings that he pitched, which was kind of the measuring stick back in those days. He always had a ton of strikeouts. But with the way he played, he also always had a ton of walks. That was the issue that kept him for so long from being a straight Major League player as opposed to bouncing back and forth between the Majors and the Minors.

I was a mess. My ego had become fragile, and I would allow situations on and off the field to dictate how I played. My inner world, or inner talk, wasn't good. I was fighting myself; I was my own worst enemy. My emotions were not just on my sleeve, they were dragging through the mud.

Everything that happened was an injustice done to me. Somebody would hit a ball, and it would affect how I pitched or an umpire would call what was clearly a strike a ball, and I'd lose my shit. Everything impacted me because everything was being done to me.

At least, that was the lie I was fighting: "Why is this happening to be me? What the hell's going on?" I'd ask myself. I was on an emotional roller coaster. It was a pity party that expressed itself in anger. The problem? I thought I had control of the uncontrollable. Of course, I didn't, that unnerved me, and being unnerved pissed me off. And around I'd go.

So, in the winter of '97, I told Dana I wasn't sure I wanted to play another season. That maybe I should call it quits, stay home, work the company I'd just bought, and provide for my family. But Dana, knowing my drive for and love of the game, and with her steady confidence, said exactly what I needed to hear.

"Look, you still love playing; I know you do. Why don't you go all in? Give it one more year. We'll be okay; we'll be fine. You just take care of what you need to take care of to get ready. Just fully invest in it with the right attitude. Give it everything you got."

Her words echoed my dad's so many years earlier: "You want to play ball, go play ball." And it was exactly what I needed to hear.

TWO THINGS CAN BE TRUE

Two things can be true at the same time. Dana was my champion; she knew I loved being a ballplayer, so she wouldn't let me quit. Dana also survived my ego by supporting me in my need to be respected and valued, so she couldn't let me quit. My dream was Dana's dream and her sacrifices to see it happen were incredible, but also necessary.

Dana gave me permission to do everything needed to succeed. But because of my brokenness, she also had to make choices that brought the most peace. So, she empowered me to chase down my dream and that was amazing. But I was ego-driven, so it was also the most selfish thing I ever did. Dana wanted me to pursue my dream, but she paid a high price because of it. Both are true.

And I am thankful. I'm thankful for her steady faith in God, her belief in me, and her sacrifice. Dana's encouragement and permission for me to give everything to baseball is the reason I didn't quit and the reason I experienced childhood dreams fulfilled.

MY WORLD

Before the season started, I called Joe. "This is it, make or break. What else can I do?" Joe, always hustling, set up a meeting with a sports psychologist out of Ohio State named Chris Stankovich. Today, working with a sports psychologist is pretty normal for athletes, but it was a fairly new concept then. Chris and I talked over the phone between the winter of '98 and up to '99, before I went to the Yankees. We had one goal: get me to perform consistently at my best.

It was all about routine and visualization. There was a poem by Robert Louis Stevenson that encapsulated my goal for routine, and I wrote it down every day for many years: "Quiet minds cannot be perplexed or frightened, but go on in fortune or in misfortune at their own private pace, like a clock during a thunderstorm."[16] I wanted to become that clock, and I wanted to make the mound a place where the fans, the weather, the stadium, the hitter couldn't enter. I called it my world. I wanted to step onto the mound, create a space, shut out the world, and perform at my best no matter what happened.

"How can you expect to be consistent for a small amount of time during a game if nothing else in your life is consistent?" Chris asked. That made sense. So, I made everything consistent, especially on game day. I had a routine for everything: what time I got up, what I ate and when, and what time I got to the ballpark. There was structure to every part of my day.

Chris also asked me to begin a journal to keep track of what I did and how I felt in the games, and then we put together a visualization process. I created a video clip in my head of me throwing the same pitch over and over and over. This video clip started with stepping onto the mound. I'd take a four-count breath and then the same as I exhaled. I'd get my sign from the catcher. Then there were three words I told myself: "posture, eyes, patience." Then I'd take another four-count breath: one, two, three, four in, and then one, two, three, four out. Then I'd let the ball go. And it worked.

For the rest of my career, that loop would play in my head before each pitch: posture, eyes, patience. That was repetition and discipline, something within my control. And that's a big deal, because the whole point is that the only control we have as humans is self-control. Every other form of control is a myth or a tragedy. The quicker I learned that I had no control over anything but myself, the better ballplayer I became. It took me a while to figure out that once I let go of that ball, I didn't have control of what happened next. I was an extremely emotional "feel player." But on the mound, those emotions didn't help; they just got in the way.

You've got to have a short memory if you're gonna succeed. You throw a pitch and they get a hit off you, you've still got to throw the next pitch. You can't lose your shit because it didn't go your way. One of the most important lessons I learned through the process of routine and visualization is I am not in control of what happens. I learned to control what I could control, but know that at the end of the day, I am not in control.

Revelation: it's called self-control and crazy enough, it's a God idea.

Self-control is the first step to freedom and one of the evidences that God is coming alive inside of us. It's the last fruit of the Holy Spirit found in Galatians 5:22-23: "But the fruit of the Spirit is love, joy, peace, forbearance, kindness, goodness, faithfulness, gentleness, and self-control." It's cool to look back and see that Scriptural truth was one of the key pieces to my success in throwing a baseball.

THE BULLPEN

In '98, thanks to Joe's hustle, I ended up going to Cleveland. I busted my ass in Spring Training like I never had before. And that's saying something. My pitching coach, Bud Black, noted it. So, on cut-down day, he fought for me. I was the last guy on the roster for their Triple-A team in Buffalo. Bud saw something in me, a potential no one else had helped me develop. Bud believed I could be most effective pitching out of the bullpen. He was the first guy who really helped me develop this role for myself within the game.

Pitching out of the bullpen is a different animal. An inning could be three minutes or thirty, and bullpen pitchers need to be ready to go in the game when their number is called. The starting pitcher has an advantage over relief pitchers. He knows when the game starts, so he can work a pre-game plan consistently. Relief pitchers, however, have to be ready at a moment's notice to compete at the highest level.

Physically I was ready, but Bud recognized my emotional volatility and took what I was learning with my new sports psychologist to help me develop the plan. Bud understood that preparing for pitching from the bullpen is the most difficult thing a pitcher can master. He taught me how to mentally get ready and stay ready coming out of the bullpen. I ended up being the closer for that team—and that changed everything.

Until Bud, I had bounced around in the Majors and the Minors for years without having any real structure. But that was the year I started killing it consistently. I ended up pitching the first ever Triple-A World Series with the Buffalo Bison. It was in Vegas. It was a cool experience; the biggest stage for Triple-A and preparation for the biggest stage of my life.

CHAPTER SEVEN

The Yankees

BAT GATE

I got to know Buster Olney when I played for Philly. He was a sports-writer who would go on to write for the *New York Times* and ESPN. At the 1999 Spring Training for the Yankees, he walked up and asked, "Jason, could you do me a favor?"

"Sure Buster, what do you need?"

"I want to get a message to somebody."

"Yeah? Who?"

"The guy who stole Albert Belle's corked bat out of the umpire's room in 1994. I need to send him a message, and word on the street is you're the guy who can get it to him." Buster was grinning.

I grinned back. "Yeah, I might know him."

He nodded appreciatively and said, "If I get permission from Baseball Commissioner Bud Selig, you think you could get him to tell me the story?"

I shrugged. "Buster, all I can do is ask."

A couple days later Buster found me in the clubhouse. "We got a green light from Selig," he said.

"One condition," I responded. "Don't release the story until after Spring Training. I'm trying to make the team and don't want any distractions."

"Done," Buster said.

I made the team and sure enough, on Opening Day, there it was: front page of the *New York Times*.

Yankee Ends Real Corker of a Mystery

Jason Grimsley, a relief pitcher in his first season with the Yankees, was among those who flocked to see the movie "Mission: Impossible" in 1996, and as he watched Tom Cruise and an accomplice crawl through an air duct to steal secret information, memories of Grimsley's own impossible mission came back to him.

Grimsley didn't steal government secrets, but he was at the center of a heist that is part of baseball lore for its audacity and ingenuity."[17]

Let's back up a little. On July 15, 1994, I was with the Cleveland Indians in a playoff race against the Chicago White Sox at Comiskey Park, their home field. I never took the team bus to games, as I always liked to get to the ballpark a bit early. I stepped out of a cab that day just as the umpires were arriving. We bullshitted as we walked together into the stadium and past the umpire room, which was located next to the visitors' locker room. I didn't think anything of it.

In the first inning, was sitting next to coach Buddy Bell in the dugout when I noticed the Chicago Manager, Gene Lamont, at home plate talking animatedly with the umpire, Dave Phillips. Gene appeared to be pointing at our left fielder, Albert Belle's, bat. Albert had been obliterating American League pitching with a .357 average and had 36 home runs that season. He was a hitter!

The umpire nodded, picked up his bat, and turned it over as if he were studying it.

"Shit," Buddy said.

I looked at him as he watched the umpire and then turned his gaze down the bench at Mike Hargrove, our manager. I followed his gaze in time to see Mike put his head down and start shaking it.

"What's going on?" I asked.

"We're screwed," Buddy said as the umpire handed the bat to a crew member, who proceeded to make his way to the umpires' dressing room for a later and closer examination.

"What?"

Buddy looked at me and said, "The bat's corked."

For those who don't follow baseball closely, a corked bat has had the barrel hollowed out and filled with cork. It makes the head of the bat lighter, which increases the speed of the swing, which leads to more control and better hits. And, of course, it's against the rules. Belle's bats were corked, which meant we were about to lose our best hitter to suspension.

"Well, shit," I said.

Then my mind kicked into high gear. Suddenly, I remembered my walk in with the umpires and where their locker room was located in relation to the visitors' clubhouse—they were pretty much next to each other.

"Buddy, I think I can get that bat." In my typical bat-shitness, I blurted it out without really having thought it through fully yet.

"What?"

The wheels were turning, and I repeated myself, doubling down. He looked at me thoughtfully for a moment, then said, "I'll be right back." He got up, walked down to Hargrove, sat down, and started talking to him. As Buddy talked, Hargrove looked down at me. Then he nodded.

Greenlight.

I went into the clubhouse to do some reconnaissance. The clubhouse had a false ceiling with removable square tiles. I estimated the distance from the clubhouse to the locked umpires' room to be at least one hundred feet but felt I could traverse the distance above the false ceiling. So, I found Gabe Capler, the visiting clubhouse manager.

"Gabe, I need a flashlight, and I need you to forget that I asked about a flashlight."

"Alright Grims," he said. Gabe was a good man.

Then I took my uniform top off, got some batting gloves, found a cork-free bat belonging to Paul Sorrento—because all of Albert Belle's bats were corked, even his batting practice bats. I put some pine tar on Sorrento's so it looked used, put the flashlight in my mouth, climbed on the desk in our manager's office, removed the false ceiling tiles, and pulled my 6' 3", 190-pound body up into the airduct system of Comiskey Park.

It wasn't a direct route. I crawled on eighteen-inch cinder blocks, crisscrossing my way there. If I slipped, it was through the ceiling tiles and the jig was up. So, I went slowly. I crawled over and under electrical wires and ducting, and water and sewer pipes, until I got to where I thought the room was. Sweating in the July heat, adrenaline flowing, I slowly lifted one of the tiles, only to lock eyes with a groundskeeper sitting on a couch. He looked at me. I looked at him, then the room, then back at him. I put my finger to my lips indicating he keep quiet. He nodded that he understood. Then I slowly put the tile back down. *Wrong room!*

By now my heart was racing 1,000 miles an hour. But one room further down, I lifted the tile. Bingo! It was the umpire's room, it was empty, and I could see the bat. I climbed down next to the refrigerator, making a small mess of sheetrock and insulation.

Dripping sweat, heart still pounding, I swapped out the offending bat with a perfectly legal and signed Paul Sorrento bat. I cleaned up the best I could, making sure I didn't leave my footprints in the dust on top of the refrigerator, and climbed back up into the ceiling. Just as I put the ceiling tile down, the door to the room opened. Every muscle in my body tensed as I sat there trying to breathe quietly through my mouth, my adrenaline firing, sure whoever it was would spot something amiss and bust me in the ceiling. But whoever it was messed around for a few minutes and left.

It took me about four and a half innings from the time the bat was confiscated to the time I rejoined the team in the dugout with the good news. Mission accomplished. I was soaked through with nervous sweat but high on pulling off the heist free and clear. Immediately after the game, which we won 3-2, the umpires let it be known that someone had stolen Albert Belle's bat out of the umpire's room and replaced it with a Sorrento! Jerry Reinsdorf, the owner of the White Sox, was pissed. He threatened in his presser that they would call in the FBI.

The next day, I was warming up pre-game along the left outfield boundary line when Mike LaValliere, the catcher for the White Sox, worked his way over to me. We called him Spanky because he looked like the famous Little Rascal of the same name. Without looking at me, he started sidestepping—all sneaky like, as though he was on a secret mission—in my direction. When he got within earshot he said, "Hey Grims, I heard you had a Mission: Impossible last night. That's awesome."

I think it was the grounds keeper who gave me up, but not to the powers that be. For many years it was a poorly kept secret between the players. But they never told. We're a brotherhood. However, the Sox organization made statements saying whoever did it would be found and prosecuted. And they only dropped the issue when our general manager, John Hart, squealed on me to the commissioner of baseball and agreed to send the Sox Belle's bat.

Meanwhile, I was summoned to see commissioner Bud Selig at the baseball offices in New York. The MLB Player's Association lawyers, Don Fehr and Michael Weiner, said, "Jason, we don't know what's going to happen. But he's probably going to fine and suspend you. Be ready for anything. But whatever happens, we're going to appeal it, so don't worry about it. We'll fight it."

I showed up in my suit and was escorted along with our legal team into Bud's office where I waited, feeling somewhat nervous. In walked Selig.

"Jason, you must be one hell of a teammate," he said as he sat down.

"Yes sir, I try to be," I said.

He looked at me seriously for a moment and waved to a chair across from him. "Sit down, son." I did. He looked at me a moment longer, then, as a smile crept into his eyes, he said, "I'm not going to fine or suspend you—just tell me the story."

So, I did. And he laughed the whole way through.

"Great story!" he said, shaking his head. Then, leaning in, "Let's keep it between us."

"Yes sir."

Belle was suspended seven games. He should have gotten ten, but I think my story saved him three. Belle thought so, too, and bought me a round of golf in thanks. And for the next five years, until Buster Olney came along, I kept it between the commissioner and myself.

THE PITCH

In November 1998, Joe set up a call with Billy Connors, a baseball advisor with the Yankees. During that call, Billy said, "Jason, I saw you pitch last year. I want to invite you to big league camp. I'm not gonna tell you you're gonna make the team by Spring Training. But if you throw the ball like you threw it last year, at some point you're gonna help this team."

The Yankees had just won the World Series. Dana and I were still struggling financially, and after the last couple of years, I'd learned I needed to get what I could when I could. "Billy, I'd absolutely love to come. Can you do me a favor? Could you get them to advance me $20,000?" I wasn't thinking my career was over. I'd had a good year previously with Bud Black, and with my newfound sense of confidence coming out of the bullpen, I knew I could still throw a baseball.

"Let me call you back," he said. When he called me back he told me, "If you make the team and we send you to Triple-A, we'll take it out of your pay. If you make the big leagues, we'll take it out of your pay. If you don't make the club, keep it." That was a good feeling: they believed in me enough to take the risk.

"Done!" I said.

When I got to Spring Training, I was ready; more ready than I'd ever been. They asked the non-roster players and the guys who weren't on the team the year before to show up a week early. They wanted us to start throwing and get comfortable with the way the Yankees went about things. It also let them get a look at us before the rest of the team arrived and everything got going.

In the Yankees Spring Training Complex in Tampa, there's a row of about eight mounds and home plates. Pitchers and catchers line up, and you throw. I was warming up and throwing fastballs, and then I threw a sinker. A sinker is a two-seam fastball. When thrown well, it's a fastball that drops just before reaching the plate, causing the batter to swing and miss. Mine moved more than most. The ball sunk so violently that it dropped below the catcher's glove and went through his legs.

"Good God," he said as he picked up the ball and threw it back. Yes, God is good. I threw the same two-seam fastball with the same results. It went through the catcher's legs—again.

Billy Connors was standing off to the side and said, "Hey Grims, that's a good split."

The catcher yelled, "It ain't a frickin split—it's a fastball!"

Billy came running over. "What?"

"It's a fastball," the catcher said again.

Billy looked at me. "Throw it again."

I did.

"Again."

I threw again.

Then he looked at me and grinned, "You're not going to throw four-seamers, or curveballs, and you're not gonna throw change-ups—from now on, you're throwing that every pitch."

With those words, Billy Connor handed me my future in baseball. I guess I was pretty good at it because I threw two-seam fastball sinkers out of the bullpen for the next seven years—and that's pretty much all I threw. It's hard to throw consistent strikes with that pitch, but I threw hard, which means those pitches were also hard to hit.

The nature of that throw is that they're gonna miss it or hit the ground. That's the idea. Even though the hitter knew what I was throwing, it didn't matter. They still had to hit it. There was no cat-and-mouse between me and the hitter. And honestly, that fits my personality. No games—just me throwing the ball as hard as I can and the batter trying to hit it.

I built the rest of my career as the pitcher who came in when guys were on base, when the starter got in trouble. I wasn't the closer, I was the set-up man. I was the guy who got us out of the inning, got us out of trouble. I handed a clean slate to the closer. Kinda like Harvey Keitel's "The Wolf" character in *Pulp Fiction*—I didn't make the mess, and I didn't stick around until the end of things, but I cleaned up in the middle.

I might pitch any inning, but as baseball has progressed, it's typically the ninth inning when the closer plays. I played before him. And I made the team outright, the 25th man on a twenty-five-man roster. But this time it was the best roster on the planet. God is good.

HALLOWED GROUND

I remember the first time I went to Yankee Stadium. It was in 1993 when I was with the Indians. The team got to New York City the night before, and I could hardly wait to see the ballpark the next day. I showed up at noon on my own, like always. They let me in the back where the deliveries arrived.

"You're early," a stadium worker noted as I walked in.

"Yeah, I know," I said.

He nodded knowingly. He'd seen it before; the wide-eyed player from a visiting team who'd come to see the mecca. I walked into the visitor clubhouse, put on my game t-shirt and my turfs. Then I walked the whole stadium. I walked the monument park that honored so many of the great Yankees and ballplayers from the past. I walked the upper deck, the outfield, then over to the home clubhouse side. I asked if I could look around and imagined what it would be like to call it home. Finally, I stood on the mound and thought about all who had stood there before me and the hitters they faced. It was just amazing. I took it all in. And I dreamed of the day . . .

MY BEST MOMENT IN BASEBALL

That first year with the Yankees was incredible. From the first game when I was baptized, then headed to the stadium for Joe DiMaggio Day where I threw two scoreless innings and we won in the eleventh inning, to the last day when I rode in a parade through the streets of NYC with my teammates and family in celebration of my first World Series: everything about playing for the Yankees was a dream. I could fill the book with stories about that year alone, but that's not what this book is about, so let's cut to the chase.

In 1999, we made the playoffs. We were playing the Texas Rangers in the best-of-five American League Division Series. Joe Torre, our manager, came to me a day before the first game and said, "Hey Jason, I just want to let you know, you're not on the active roster. We got you as an alternate. You're still gonna dress, but you're not gonna play."

I nodded and said, "I understand." And I was fine with it. We won the series in three games. The Boston Red Sox were our next playoff opponent. This was a best-of-seven series to claim the American League pennant. Same thing, a day before the series kicked off, Joe Torre found me and said, "We're gonna leave it like it is."

I was less than fine with it this time, especially after he started another pitcher who hadn't been playing well and went on to give up eight runs in two innings. The Yankees had paid a premium to have that pitcher on their roster and, to me, it felt like that might be playing into the decision.

But Joe was the manager, I was the player. So, I nodded. "Alright, Joe." We ended up winning that series in five games. We were in the World Series against Atlanta. That was the dream for this East Texas kid, but I hadn't played in a month.

The day before we left for Atlanta, the pitchers were practicing bunting because while we don't hit in the American League, the

National League (NL) doesn't have a designated hitter (DH) rule. And since Atlanta was the home team for the Series, the NL rules would apply. No DH, so pitchers had to hit. I was standing behind the batting cage on the field when Joe walked up.

"Hey Grims, I just want to let you know, we're leaving the roster like it is."

He turned to leave, and I said, "Joe, that's bullshit."

"What?" he asked.

"You heard me—it's bullshit."

Joe looked at me and asked sincerely, "Why is it bullshit, Jason?"

"It's simple, Joe. You don't want to piss off somebody making five million, so you'd rather piss off somebody making $350,000. But both of us know the other pitcher isn't playing well enough for you to start him in a game in the World Series. It's not gonna happen. If you do put him in, these guys out here are gonna quit because they know the game's over. But if you put me in a ballgame, these guys are gonna think they have a chance to win a ballgame. And there ain't a frickin thing you could tell me that would change my mind!" I was hot as I finished, "That's why it's bullshit, Joe." After that, I started to walk off.

"Hey!" Joe said.

"What?"

"I haven't made my mind up yet!"

"Whatever!"

Then I went home and said to Dana, "Honey, we might not be going to Atlanta."

"Why?" She asked.

"I just pissed off the manager."

Dana didn't say anything. She knew me, knew I spoke my mind, and knew there wasn't anything she could do but ride it out.

The next day at the clubhouse as we were getting ready to leave, Joe came by my locker. "I need to see you in my office."

"Shit, here it is," I thought. I went in and sat down.

Joe looked at me as though I hadn't verbally accosted him the day before. "You're active; you're on the roster."

I also acted like nothing had happened and said, "Alright, Joe."

I got up to leave and Joe said, "Jason, I'll have you know, money never had anything to do with it."

I nodded, "Alright, Joe." After all, Joe was the manager, and I was the player.

Then I got on the phone with Dana. "We're going to Atlanta," I said, grinning into the phone. Then I called my family and let them know they needed to pay close attention. "I've got spikes on and I'm active—there's a chance I might pitch," I said.

"I might pitch" is an overstatement. If you know anything about that '99 Yankees team, you know the chances of me seeing the field were slim to none; our starting four were ridiculous. We had Orlando Hernandez, Andy Pettitte, David Cone, and Roger Clemens, who was arguably the best pitcher of our generation. And while I'm on the subject of great pitchers, Atlanta had John Smoltz, Tom Glavine, and Greg Maddux. They were pretty solid as well.

The first two games were in Atlanta. We won the first game 5-1. Hernandez started and Mariano closed the game. It wasn't even close. In the second game, Dave Cone, who had pitched a perfect game earlier that season, started. Just so we understand, in over 150 years of Major League baseball and over 218,400 games played, there have been 23 official perfect games.[18] Dave was pretty good. Ramiro Mendoza came in for the eighth inning and Jeff Nelson came in the ninth and finished it out. We won again.

Games 3 and 4 were home games. And we still had the same elite pitchers, so my chances were getting smaller by the minute. I was okay with it. I mean, I wanted out there, but just being active was a dream come true. Andy Petite started the third game. Somehow, he gave up four runs in the first two innings. In the third inning, he gave up another, and we were down five to nothing.

Suddenly they called down, "Grims, you're in."

There have only been two times where I pretty much floated to the mound. The first I've told you about—when I pitched my first game in the Major Leagues in Canada. You remember, the one where my parents hammed it up with Donald Sutherland. The second time it happened was Game 3 in the World Series. My feet never touched the turf.

When they opened up those bullpen gates in the old Yankee Stadium and I came into the ballgame, the realization hit me in the mouth. Full go, the fans, the history of the players who'd come before, the team, the game, the dreams of me as a kid—every kid. This was the World Series. It was fantasy come to life.

Any athlete who says they don't pay attention to the intense reality of a game situation is full of shit. This was the World Series and millions of people around the world were watching. There were fifty thousand people in the stands, and every eye was on me. Everything I'd ever dreamed about as a little kid was playing out in this moment. And I was aware of it all.

Nervous doesn't even come close to what I felt as I walked to the mound. You couldn't have driven a greasy peg up my ass with a sledge hammer. Then I noted how Joe Torre and pretty much the whole team were waiting for me at the mound. Our catcher, Joe Girardi, was there, as well as our first baseman, Tino Martinez. And our second baseman, our short stop, Derek Jeter, and our third baseman, Scott Brosius.

I started thinking, "They've been here before. They've done it.

They've already succeeded at the highest level. And I am, Jason Grimsley, a journeyman. And they're all looking at me. And in this moment, it's up to me. There's one out and a man on base, and it's up to me."

And then I was standing next to Joe. He was holding the ball, and as I walked up to him, I thought, "He's gonna impart some wisdom on me. He's gonna talk to me a little about the situation or give me some advice." But he just looked me in the eye and without breaking eye contact, handed me the ball and said, "Here you go." Then he walked away. But I heard him loud and clear. Without word he'd said, "Alright, son, your ass wrote a check, let's see if you can cash it."

"Alright, Joe," I thought. Joe was the manager; I was the player. And this was my time.

I stepped onto the mound and into my world, my universe, the quiet. I centered myself and all nervousness left me. Then I played the game I loved. I pitched like I'd been doing it my whole life. For three innings, I didn't allow any runs scored. We tied the ballgame and ended up winning in the tenth on a walk-off home run.

Everything about that game was surreal, including the atmosphere after the game in the clubhouse. After a win, in the regular season or otherwise, all the sons of players could come join us in the clubhouse. At that time, Hunter was almost five and John was three. They came running into the clubhouse, and as was typical, Hunter ran past with a wave and a "Hi, Dad," as he headed for the arcade games with the other boys in an adjacent room. But John didn't go with him. Instead, he pushed through the thirty or so reporters that crowded my locker, all looking for the perfect soundbite for their feature story. And that night I was their feature story.

I hadn't faced a hitter in twenty-eight days. I hadn't competed throughout the whole playoffs. And then, I threw three scoreless innings in a World Series. The reporters moved aside, making room for John until he reached me. I picked him up as I continued to answer questions.

"You weren't on the active roster the first few rounds of the playoffs, and you hadn't pitched in some time. What was going through your mind?" Susan Walden, of the YES Network, asked.

I started to answer, then we all heard Joe Torre screaming as he entered the locker room. "Way to go, Jason Grimsley! Way to go!"

Everyone smiled. Then I started to answer her question, but John kept grabbing my face and trying to turn it toward his. He wanted me to look at him.

"Wait a minute, buddy, hang on a second. Daddy's trying to talk to these people," I said.

I started to answer again, but he kept at it.

"John-John, let me talk to Miss Susan." But he wouldn't stop, so finally I said, "Excuse me for a second," and I turned and looked him in the eyes.

He patted me on the cheek and said, "Way to go, Daddy, way to go." And I started to cry. That was my best moment in baseball—just holding John and him patting me on the cheek and saying, "Way to go." It wasn't just the success on the field, being able to help the team, or the accolades after. It was sharing all of it with John-John and the rest of my family—Dana, the kids, my parents, and my Nanny—who not only celebrated that win but also the next, when we won the World Series.

I've often been asked what it was like to be in the stadium that day. Euphoric, heady, rapturous. No word quite captures it—the brotherhood of that moment, the sense of completion and having successfully arrived at the ultimate finish line. And with thousands of thrilled fans alongside you and millions more behind the cameras—yeah, it's not the whole story of a life, but wow, what an experience. Yet, as amazing as that moment was, it was nothing next to celebrating later with those I love and who love me.

It was that much more amazing because my family was there and able to experience it with me, including the experience of being celebrated by The Big Apple as Dana and my kids joined me on the float in the ticker-tape parade. Good God, New York knows how to celebrate its team's successes!

THE YANKEES

I loved everything about playing for the Yankees, from the people who helped in the stadium to the police officers who worked security. I especially appreciated Sergeant Lenny Tobie, who headed up security at Yankee Stadium when I was there. He was always good to me and my family. I loved the clubhouse guys and all the kids in the clubhouse.

And I loved Yankees fans. They are passionate. When you played against them, it was rough as they were merciless, but when you wore that uniform, it was unbelievable. They even know everybody who *has* played for them. I couldn't walk the city without someone noting I was a Yank. And they have lots of famous fans, which was fun.

Biff Henderson, the famous stage manager for *Late Night with David Letterman*, was one such fan. I let him hit off me in Spring Training and we hit it off. After we won the Pennant, I went on Letterman to do one of his famous Top Ten lists. Biff came up to me before the show and with a thumbs up said, "You're gonna do five."

I met Mark Tremonti, the lead guitar player for Creed, through a mutual friend in 2000. The album *Human Clay* had just hit, and I loved it. Plus, the band members were Yankees fans. They'd done a show somewhere in NYC and wanted to come to a game and see the field. They asked if I would talk with Joe Torrie to make it happen.

I did and Torre said, "Sure, no problem."

What I heard was, "Yeah, show them the whole place. Hell, take them on the field." But apparently that's not what "Sure, no problem" meant. Joe thought I'd take them in the dugout and *show* them the field. Nope, we all got in the cage and hit a little, and they were playing catch when George Steinbrenner saw it and blew a gasket. I got my ass in a crack for that. And when lead singer Scott Stapp and Mark found out, they felt pretty bad.

"Don't worry about it. I'll take the ass-chewing; it's not that big a deal," I said.

After the 2000 World Series, which we won again, they invited me to a show in Baton Rouge. I brought my brother-in-law Tommy and his wife Diane with me, and it was awesome. We went backstage and ended up hanging out with the band and playing ping-pong. That's where Mark and I really connected.

That's the thing about being a Yankee: you find yourself a part of baseball at its core.

I got to meet so many incredible people and, to this day, I feel that same comradery. A few years back I went to one of the Old Timers games hosted at the stadium. I showed up, saw the guys, and it was like no time had passed. We fell right back into it, messing around, joking, telling stories, hugging, laughing, and having a good time.

Ron Guidry, Mariano, Bernie, and Mickey Rivers were there; Lou Piniella, who managed while I was playing, was there; Johnny Damon and Jason Giambi too. I connected with guys I played against but who also played for the Yankees when I wasn't there. It's a brotherhood, and if you wore the uniform, you are part of the brotherhood forever.

It's about the history, but also about the owner, George Steinbrenner. He is one of the greatest men I've ever met. That man would come down the clubhouse at home games with regularity and ask us if everything was alright or if we needed anything. He's the only owner

I ever experienced that with. He loved his players. He expected you to do your job, but if you weren't doing your job, he truly wanted to know why so he could help fix it. There's a reason the Yankees were who they were. And it was a privilege and honor to play for them and for George Steinbrenner.

CHAPTER EIGHT

The Journey to Salvation

THE FIRST TIME I GOT SAVED

I want to back up a bit to early 1999, which was Spring Training with the Yankees leading up to our back-to-back World Series championships. It was when so many good things all came together. Deep inside, I knew I needed God. I had a front row seat to my sins, and I'd always respected the church, but to need God was an admonition of weakness—something I wasn't interested in.

I thought it was good that Dana went to church, but I'd successfully resisted for years. Dana attended every Sunday morning and Wednesday night for Bible study. She was pretty involved with the church. And she was on me a lot. She wanted me to believe in God or to at least behave like I did. She knew some of my sins and lived with my ego. She knew I needed God, and she also needed me to need God.

"You need to connect with God," she'd say. So, I would go with her sometimes, but I went for the same reasons I'd gone as a kid: I was just trying to appease her. I'd even go to a team chapel once and a while just so I could tell her and get her off my back. Dana will tell you now, pressuring me to go to church so God could fix me probably wasn't the best thing for us. She says that if she could do it over, she would pray for me, seek counsel, and kindly, steadily confront my heart issues without an agenda to change behaviors—all for the purpose of seeing me set free.

But that's the kind of wisdom gained through enduring the heartbreaking struggle she walked through. That's the kind of thing said in hindsight, after you have walked through the shit. And I put her through the shit. I knew it, even in my brokenness, and I wanted to do better. That's a good desire, but there was a problem. If "doing better" is the fruit of a life surrendered to the love of God, that's beautiful. But if "doing better" is about trying harder to prove something? Yeah, that isn't sustainable.

So, during that first Spring Training with the Yankees, I went with her to church on Easter to appease her or try to prove something, but I also had a sincere desire to do better. I knew I needed something. My emotional and spiritual state was poor. We'd been bouncing around for three years, we had two boys and Dana was pregnant with our girl, and I felt all the responsibilities that came with that. I wondered what our future held, too. So, I was suddenly open to God in ways I hadn't been in the past.

It was a nice service, a big production. I'd seen it before, but now it made sense. Jesus died so we could be set free from our sins, so we could know His love and experience His forgiveness, and so we could awaken to grace by faith in Christ Jesus. I wanted forgiveness, a clean slate. I wanted to "do better." I accepted Jesus into my life and my heart expanded once again.

Life is a journey, and we're making decisions along the way—decisions for life, decisions to numb pain. Along the way we get revelation—not the whole story but another part of the story. And that first time I prayed for salvation was a huge part of my story.

THE PRODIGAL SON

When I look at most of my life, I see two halves corresponding with the parable of the Prodigal Son that Jesus told in Luke 15.

If you remember, this parable was about a father with two sons. The youngest asked for and received his inheritance, a large sum of money. Then he left home to spend it in every self-centered, self-destructive way possible. The young fella became his own master, and he was a poor one. Eventually, he ran out of money and fell on hard times, ending up as a servant for a harsh master. His job was to feed the pigs, and Scripture notes that they ate better than he did. In those dark and desperate days, he remembered how his father's servants were treated kindly. He realized his father was a good master—better than the master he served. So, he decided to return home, ask for forgiveness, and request a position as a servant in his father's house. And this is where the story gets good:

> But while he was still a long way off, his father saw him and felt compassion, and ran and embraced him and kissed him. And the son said to him, "Father, I have sinned against heaven and before you. I am no longer worthy to be called your son." But the father said to his servants, "Bring quickly the best robe, and put it on him, and put a ring on his hand, and shoes on his feet. And bring the fattened calf and kill it, and let us eat and celebrate. For this my son was dead, and is alive again; he was lost, and is found." And they began to celebrate.[19]

I love this story; I can identify with the young fella. I think most people feel the same way at some point in their life. He felt unworthy to be a son for a lot of reasons. He'd screwed up and hurt people. But the father forgave and restored him and then threw a party! And what's most amazing is that the father restored him to sonship.

The first half of my life, whether I realized it or not, I was the prodigal. I was the kid who lived wild and loose; I was my own god, and I chased my selfish ambitions with reckless abandon. But like that prodigal, I eventually found myself desperate in my relationships and in my own heart.

That Easter morning in 1999, I was a prodigal come home, and I experienced God's love and forgiveness and salvation. I felt a sense of peace and joy—felt set free! And I was overwhelmed with thankfulness.

THE GOOD MASTER

We are all God's kids, and He is our Father. But many of His kids never truly get to know Him as Dad—most of His kids know Him only as Master. That's not wrong, but it's not the whole story. God is a good master. But even more amazing, God is our good and loving Father. And that was the whole story Jesus was telling in this parable. The prodigal returned to serve a good master, only to discover his father in a way he never knew him before he left home.

On that Easter Day, I was a prodigal son returning home to a good Master. I had spent most of my life serving myself, and I was a poor master. Like the prodigal, I had chased my ambitions, my ego, my ideas of what it meant to be free. All lies. I had served the harsh master of my reputation and was stumbling in the dark. Like the prodigal, I had some of the same types of friends—people who took me places I shouldn't have gone and introduced me to things that would enslave me. And I was confused, selfish, and frustrated. My wife was lonely and hurt, and with good reason. I knew I needed saving. That Easter, just like the prodigal son, I had an epiphany: God is a good Master.

Now this is a good epiphany, a good and true revelation. Anyone who's enslaved to their ego, fears, insecurities, and sins knows they need to serve a better master than the one they are serving. And discovering God is a trustworthy and good Master who can save us from the broken masters we are enslaved to? Well, that's a really good thing.

I think the first step to freedom is found in the thought that God is a good Master. And that's the freedom I got that Easter Sunday. I realized I was a lost son lost struggling in my own brokenness, and I repented.

Revelation: I could see Jesus as a Savior who would die for me.

Jesus laying His life down for me made sense where it hadn't before. It ordered my disordered world. The Christian faith gave language to my drive for excellence, gave significance to my sense of self, and provided a sense of purpose greater than me. It provided a road map to "doing better."

Was it the whole story? No. It was simply a new beginning; I was a prodigal headed home. I was a prodigal with a forgiving Father. Were all the broken places within me immediately healed? No. It was a new beginning. It was my best yes within the context of my understanding. That's something worth noting. All we can do is give our best yes.

God is always with us, reminding us of His kindness, speaking to us, giving us the understanding that we need along the way. God speaks to us in the language of our understanding. And on Easter Sunday 1999, I said yes to God. I said yes to the Master.

On that day I began a journey home; I decided I would become a servant in the house of the greatest, kindest, and most loving Master. And for the next several years, that would be the context of my relationship with God.

I liked the order. I liked the sense of right and wrong. I liked the clear definition of what Jesus did on a cross. And I liked the rules. They were good rules, righteous rules. Rules I could apply so I might "do better." I was a disciplined man who excelled at performing. And that word, *perform*, is perfect if you're in a servant-master relationship, but it can be devastating when used in the relationship between a son and his father. After that Easter, when I knew Jesus as my Savior and Master, there was peace for a time between Dana and me.

THE OLDER BROTHER

God is a good and kind Master in a world full of cruel masters. Whether it's our own ego, addiction, broken family dynamics, shame, or controlling people or organizations, we all know the oppressive experience of serving cruel masters. But God isn't like that.

And that Easter Sunday I gave my heart to the good Master, still not knowing my good Father, still living and thinking in the context of a slave. And in many ways, I began a journey into the next season of my life still as a slave, except this time I slaved for God. That may not sound bad, but there was a second son in the prodigal son parable, an older brother. The story of the prodigal son isn't about just one son.

> Now his older son was in the field, and as he came and drew near to the house, he heard music and dancing. And he called one of the servants and asked what these things meant. And he said to him, "Your brother has come, and your father has killed the fattened calf, because he has received him back safe and sound." But he was angry and refused to go in. His father came out and entreated him, but he answered his father, "Look, these many years I have served you, and I never disobeyed your command, yet you never

gave me a young goat, that I might celebrate with my friends. But when this son of yours came, who has devoured your property with prostitutes, you killed the fattened calf for him!"

And he said to him, "Son, you are always with me, and all that is mine is yours. It was fitting to celebrate and be glad, for this your brother was dead, and is alive; he was lost, and is found."[20]

Much of the second half of my life, at least until the last several years, I became the older brother. I was a performer earning my way. And being an older brother can be even more devastating and heartbreaking than being a prodigal. You see, the older brother was like the younger in that he served a master, and yet he didn't truly know his father. Notice what he said to his dad: "Look! all these years I've been slaving for you." Slaving is ultimately what happens in a performance-based relationship with God.

ON FIRE BUT GETTING COLDER

That year with the Yankees, I was on fire for God. I wanted to know God like I knew baseball. Dana was actually upset with me because I spent more time with the Bible than with her. I loved God and what He had done for me and wanted to change the world for Him.

And it was a year of amazing experiences: we won the World Series and I experienced New York as a Yankee, which meant being recognized and cheered and adored. It meant I could eat in any restaurant and be celebrated. The ego-stroking of my new-found fame was intoxicating. Hell, I did Letterman and hung out with famous people. It was truly exciting—and also all about me.

When everything in life is self-focused, you can get sideways fast.

I started drifting further and further from a passion to know and serve God toward the old addiction to be seen as the man, the bad dude. I moved from those brief, freeing moments where I felt the affection and kindness of God, where I sensed His grace and mercy, to being a lip-service Christian.

The next year I got a little further away. I'd go to the occasional Bible study, but I was reading it less and my zeal for God waned. I was doing pretty good on my own. At least, that's how I began to live and think. It's hard to be humble when everything you do is about performing and you're successful—or at least you appear to be. And that was my life in those years. I was the successful Christian ballplayer at home and that good-looking, good-time, man's man successful ballplayer on the road. My days were filled with accolades and adoration.

The fact is, I'd seen God's miracles in my life both before and after I called Him Lord and Savior. I should have died more times than I've already mentioned; whether it was bicycle accidents or near-drowning as a kid, or motorcycle wrecks where I almost bled out. There were so many times when God walked beside me and saved me. But now I knew it was Him all along. Yet something was still missing, and the drive to "do better," even if it was for Him, wasn't enough to make me do better.

I didn't see it at the time, but God was still carrying me along, and He had more for me than to "do better." Now I can look back and realize He was saying, "I've got something better for you, a freedom that isn't performance-based, a salvation that can't be earned." But I would almost die before I finally discovered it. I would have to exhaust my own ego.

You see, performance can bring striving and earning to Christianity. Like the older brother, you can slave. But it won't serve you. Instead, you will find yourself bumping up against the very Master you think you serve. The older brother couldn't bring himself to join the party for his returned brother. He stood outside the celebration, cut off from life, angry and alone.

And that's what I did over the next couple of years. I was the older brother slaving for a master, earning my way into righteousness, growing ever-more arrogant, and becoming angrier and lonelier along the way. And eventually that self-righteous "do better" approach to life will lead to unrighteousness.

It's crazy how you can take your dedication to God and turn it into something that's all about you. Everything was about what I could do for God as opposed to simply receiving what God has already done for me. I grew cold in faith and bitter. I went right back into the way I was living before. But now I did it with a reckless arrogance that, looking back now, scares the shit out of me.

During that time, I had a lot of success on the field and that made it easier to think I could get away with anything. So, I drifted away from God and toward the end of my career. And especially after I got involved in drugs and alcohol. I mean, it became a problem—one that I had to hide from everyone. And once you start hiding shit, well, there's always more shit to hide.

I got involved with a woman. It wasn't about love; it was a sickness, an addiction to destructive behavior. I was with the Kansas City Royals, playing an away game in Cleveland. Dana called my hotel room; the girl answered the phone. Then Dana called the club house. It broke Dana's heart. And that was something I truly didn't want to do. I loved her. I was so ashamed, so angry at myself for hurting her. I felt lower than a slug. I went to my manager and told him, "I gotta go home." That's something you don't do. I flew home to Louisiana, walked in the door, and she was broken.

I think there were two reasons Dana didn't ask for a divorce: She has always believed in a God who redeems, reconciles, and restores. And she never doubted that I loved her; she knew I was broken. Even in her pain, she understood that I never did anything out of malice toward her. Even though she couldn't understand the hidden nature of my brokenness, and even though I hurt her, she knew I wanted to do better. She believed that I would try to do better, to fix it.

At the time, we just moved forward—limped along—as I tried to make amends, as I tried to stay one more year in baseball. But there was a growing list of things I couldn't control. I know that sounds weak—and that's the point: I was weak. The man who couldn't show any weakness, the self-made big-time ball player, a man not to be messed with, the Christian man—couldn't seem to control any aspect of his personal life.

This is the real stuff; this is real life.

I think we do things to survive. We do things out of our brokenness. I know that was the case for me. My "never show weakness" approach to life was crushing me, and I did everything I could to medicate the pain; whatever I could do to survive. I became a façade of the older brother, striving and presenting a good front to the world. But inside, I was on the road to destruction.

The beautiful thing about the gospel is it actually requires weakness. But the weakness must be admitted; there must be a surrender. And while I understood this, I still couldn't fully participate in it. You see, I could not show vulnerability. I hid my pain and shame. I'd rather die than expose it. And it was killing me and deeply hurting everyone I loved. And no one more so than Dana.

Success had only exacerbated the issue. But it was also the last bastion I clung to, the last fortress of my crumbling ego. And then it was ripped from me.

The first time I committed my life to Christ, I was on fire, but I thought there was something that I had to do to deserve the salvation. I thought, "I gotta go earn it." But that's religion, and it will mess you up. You'll end up like the older brother.

The second time I gave my life to Christ, I learned that I'm not earning anything, I'm just receiving. I am learning how to receive love, grace, and mercy. I think that's the gospel Jesus walked the planet to share—and more to the point, He walked next to me so I might discover it. The good news is He is with me, regardless of what I deserve. I think the gospel will empower you to look in the mirror and like what you see because it's not about what you earned, but what God has done.

CHAPTER NINE

The Beginning of the End

HGH

HGH is not as potent as steroids, but the idea is the same. It's a performance-enhancing drug (PED) that promotes speed of recovery and muscle growth. HGH is a synthetic drug that mimics the growth hormone that "fuels childhood growth and helps maintain tissues and organs throughout life." But when we hit middle age, the gland that naturally produces this hormone gradually produces less.[21] And so, athletes, especially older ones, supplement this hormone.

In 2004, the league began testing for steroids. So, I stopped using steroids but continued to use HGH. It helped me build muscle, develop strength, and recover faster after a workout. In 2006, after having played a game the night before, I was awakened to FBI and IRS agents on my front lawn with proof I'd been using HGH. There's often a feeling of relief when you've been doing something you shouldn't and you're finally caught. But I think that only happens if you have a guilty conscience.

I didn't have a guilty conscience. To be honest, I still don't. Not about that, anyway. Do performance-enhancing drugs belong in baseball? No. But between 1993 and 2004, when I played, steroids and HGH became an unregulated part of the game.

MLB Pitcher David Wells said that during that time "somewhere between 25 and 40 percent of all Major Leaguers [were] juiced."[22] In an interview with *Sports Illustrated* and in his tell-all book *Juiced*, Jose Canseco claimed about 80 percent of players used steroids; he was well-known for using steroids throughout his career and encouraging others to do the same.[23] Alex Rodriguez allegedly tested positive for steroids in 2003—the same year when he was American League MVP. In February 2009, Rodriguez admitted to taking PEDs between 2001 and 2003.[24] In January 2010, after years of dodging allegations of PED use, Mark McGwire admitted that he had used steroids and HGH off and on for over a decade, including in 1998, when he set the single-season home run record.[25]

I had made a twenty-year career as a journeyman, the 25th man. I was in the League by the skin of my teeth and sheer force of will. And by the support of Dana and all the other people who encouraged me along the way. For two decades, I had been cut and fought my way back time and again.

While it was true for every athlete, I knew better than most that I was a commodity. I was disposable, a piece of meat, and the League didn't give two shits about me. Just as soon as I couldn't perform, I was gone. It was all over the moment I couldn't perform. And during a time when so much of the league used PEDs at some point, I didn't view it as right or wrong but simply as something I had to do to compete.

Growing up, right or wrong was mostly about fairness. And rules were like the speed limit—meant to be pushed and ignored when arbitrary, and especially if ungoverned. We didn't talk about it directly, but everyone top to bottom knew PEDs were in baseball. So, to me, taking HGH was like driving with the flow of traffic. Was I speeding? Yes. But so was everyone else. So, how could I have a guilty conscience?

I am not saying I was right. I was wrong. I broke the rules. But in my mind, I got caught speeding. But to the FBI, I was Johnny Cash in Reno.

THE THREE LETTER AGENCIES

Should I have gone with them when they showed up at my door? Probably not. But I didn't think I had a choice. And later, in front of a grand jury, I was able to explain why. And that hour with a grand jury restored some of my lost faith in the justice system.

I can't really talk about what was said in front of the grand jury, but I can tell you there was no condescension or political agenda. There was no hotshot FBI agent trying to make a name for himself, willing to threaten, extort, coerce, strong arm, lie, intimidate, badger, shakedown, or blackmail me into achieving his objective. Nope—just honest questions with a sincere desire to learn the truth, the whole story. They simply wanted to know what happened. They listened and engaged; they were genuine, and it was cathartic to simply tell them what I knew.

My amazing lawyer and an even better man, Ed Novak, said, "Jason, just be honest; tell the whole truth and nothing but the truth, and you'll be good." He was right, but a year earlier, that was not the case with the lead FBI agent. But I'm getting ahead of myself.

I don't know if I was the only player getting HGH from my out-of-state source (I doubt it), but I was the only one who paid with checks. Why didn't I use cash? Well, first, HGH isn't heroin. Doctors prescribe this stuff; possessing it isn't illegal. Second, I had no idea shipping it across state lines was a federal crime—until the FBI showed up at the house with the HGH kit I'd ordered.

My brother-in-law and sister-in-law, my niece, my three kids, Dana, and the nanny were home. At the time, home was Arizona—I was playing for the Diamondbacks. It was 9 a.m., and I'd gotten in late the night before from a game. So, I was still in bed. My brother-in-law came in and said, "Jason, you've got a package. They want you to sign for it."

"Tell them you're me and sign for it," I said.

He came back a few minutes later, looking a little more serious, and said, "Jason, they said they need to see you."

I got to the door and Dana was already there, standing with a couple of suits. There were four or five cars in the driveway and along the road. I don't know how many agents, but I quickly surmised this wasn't a delivery.

"Are you Jason Grimsley?" a suited man asked.

"Yep."

He noted the package he held and said, "We need to talk to you."

I noted the package, nodded, and stepped out the door onto the front porch as Dana said, "Jason, you need to call Joe." I nodded to her and then gave my attention to the man.

The guy was an uncompromising asshole, the kind of fella motivated less by injustice and more by an opportunity to further his career. But I didn't know that yet.

"We can do this one of two ways," he said. "You can come in with us to talk, or we can come into your house, handcuff you, and zip tie everybody else. Then we'll tear the place apart." He looked at me until I understood he would make good on his threat. "Your choice."

That's not a choice. There was no way in hell I was gonna let them come into the house, restrain Dana and my family, and scare the kids.

"I'll go talk with you."

Dana was pissed when I told her I was going with them. But she hadn't heard the threat he'd made. "Trust me on this, Dana. I can't tell you why, but I'm gonna go talk to him. Call Joe."

In hindsight, I don't know what I could have done differently. But later, the FBI would spin the following interview as a confession—not of my own use of HGH; I never denied that. But they would make it seem as though I gave them names of other players who used PEDs on that day.

I didn't.

What did happen that day was that I began to learn the FBI isn't just in the justice business—they also muck around in politics. Politics is about good press, and convicting Jason Grimsley isn't good press. But convicting Barry Bonds and some of the biggest names in baseball? That's good press. It was also the day I began to learn they'd do whatever they needed to do to me to produce those names.

They drove me to a hotel where they had a room set up with cameras and microphones and recording devices. (Yeah, it was like a movie—except this wasn't a movie.) They let me know they had my HGH source and knew about every purchase I'd made from him. Then, hanging the end of my career and jail time over my head, they accused me of selling PEDs to other players and threatened to charge me if I didn't tell them who I was selling to. But I wasn't selling. I bought enough for my season and that's what I told them.

"Guys, the HGH was for me. There are likely other players who take it, but I have never sold or ever seen anyone take anything."

"What about Manny Ramirez, Roger Clemens, Andy Pettite?"

"Guys, I have never seen anyone take anything."

"What about Miguel Tejada, Brian Roberts, Jay Gibbons?"

"How many times do I have to say this: I have never seen anyone take anything."

"What about Barry Bonds?" They had a hard-on for Barry Bonds.

"Guys, I have never, ever, seen someone take PEDs. Period. Full stop."

I said this over and over. But they wouldn't leave off.

"You're in big trouble, Jason. You're facing jail time, but maybe we can help if you just give us some names."

Even if I'd known something, I wouldn't have told them. But the fact is, I didn't know anything, at least not for certain. "Guys, do I have suspicions? Sure. And I could assume with you about anyone, but I've never personally seen anybody do anything."

Finally, they switched gears. Still hanging the end of my career and jail time over my head, they asked if I would be willing to wear a wire. But it wasn't really an ask. "This is what you're gonna do. You're gonna get information recorded so we can catch other players."

I didn't want to take the wire, but at this point, I did want to get out of there. Finally, they took me back to my house. On the way the lead agent told me, "Don't call your agent, don't call a lawyer, and you can't talk to teammates. If you do, we will arrest you, we'll out you, and your career will be over."

As soon as I got home, I called Joe, then my lawyer, and then I threw my wire away. The FBI had nothing on anyone but me. They could prove I'd taken HGH and earlier DECA (steroids), but they were fishing on everyone else and using me as bait. And I refused to be their bait.

For the next few weeks, I took that agent's calls and waited for him to make good on his threats. Every conversation was the same: "We'll out you and end your career if you don't help us entrap your teammates."

I felt helpless and absolutely miserable. I wasn't ready for my career to end, and definitely not like this, but I remained unwilling to play the role they had assigned me. Those weeks were the beginnings of a hell that I had spent years running from finally catching up with me. It was a hell that would torment me for years after; a hell I'd eventually surrender to with a gun in the woods.

THE END

I hadn't given the FBI anything they could use, and their patience was growing thin. Then the Giants came to town. Barry Bonds played for the Giants. And they wanted Barry in the worst way. On game day, the agent called and asked if I was going to cooperate. He wanted me to wear a wire and somehow cozy up to Bonds and get him to admit to PED use.

I'd had enough, so I bit back: "Look, you've been hanging the end of my career and jail time over my head for too long, so I'm gonna take one of those options off the table. I'm gonna retire, 'cause I'll leave baseball before I wear a wire for you idiots. Do what you're gonna do, but don't call me again."

I planned on quitting that day, after the game. I went to the ballpark that night heavy-hearted but also feeling like I was finally in control of my own future again. That lasted till halfway through the game, when I looked up to see my face and name plastered across every screen in the stadium: "Diamondback's pitcher Jason Grimsley is being investigated for PED use by FBI."

It was all over ESPN—and every other news channel. I don't remember much else of the game, my last game. I walked off the field numb; my past, present, and future roaring in my ears. I remember the rest of the night as though I was watching from outside my body. In the clubhouse after the game, there was anger. The owner was there, and he was pissed.

I called a team meeting. "Guys, this is what happened. I ordered some HGH; they got me in a pinch. They wanted me to wear a wire;

to talk to you guys, to get you guys on tape. They wanted me to entrap Bonds. I told them to go screw themselves. Told them I wouldn't do that to you or my family, so I'm out. They outed me. I'm done. I quit. I'm going to the house."

Then I left baseball forever. When I walked out of that stadium, I walked away from a twenty-two-year career—not in celebration, but under the condemnation of the sports world and a shadow of lies and accusations and fear of potential legal retribution.

Twenty-two years and it was over in a moment.

I still had self-respect, and over time—when the truth started coming to light—the respect of most of my teammates. But in the days and years after, I was alone. Desperately alone. It was the hardest way to leave baseball. The game itself is something I love. It was my life, and suddenly it was ripped from me.

At the end of the day, the FBI didn't want Jason Grimsley; they wanted Barry Bonds, they wanted Roger Clemens, and they wanted baseball itself. And eventually, they got it. There were over 150 suspensions in the Major and Minor Leagues.

I DIDN'T DO IT

I heard the MLB player reps had a meeting a few days later. One of them stood up and said, "Jason just needs to keep his frickin mouth shut."

But the union rep and lawyer, Michael Weiner, stood up for me. "I've got respect for Jason. You don't know what that man has been going through. You don't know what he did or what this is costing him, so shut the fuck up!"

I appreciate what he said, 'cause not too many in those early days had my back. The players who knew me—players who really knew me—wouldn't have believed it, but the rest of the world did. I understood and still do understand that it's hard to know the truth in the middle of something. And in this case especially because so many half-truths and bold-faced lies were being propagated by the FBI through the media. So, when I would read articles where players or friends spoke the truth, it was encouraging.

Former Minor League catcher Jeremy Jones said, "I played with a lot of guys that tried [steroids]. . . . It was all over the place, even in the Minors. And you let one person do it, and everybody is going to be doing it to stay up with everybody. That was baseball's problem."[26] And I'm thankful for friends like Chris Mihlfeld, who helped me rehabilitate from Tommy John surgery in 2005 and was my strength and conditioning coach from 2001 through 2005. Chris told ESPN, "I could never imagine that Jason Grimsley would come out and bring names up and point fingers at players. He's a player's player. He is a man's man."[27]

And he was correct—I didn't "out names" or "point fingers." And he was also correct on the whole "player's player" and "man's man" thing. I'm proud that I never outed anyone, even when I had legitimate suspicions. I'm proud that I didn't wear a wire. And as painful as it was to lose my career that way, I'm grateful that I didn't play any active role in ending others' careers.

But that doesn't mean I got everything right. I had so many friends and coaches and trainers who were friends, and because of the intense political nature of the witch hunt, their very connection to me affected some of their careers. I have regrets. Especially that I didn't reach out to those players I had history with whose lives it affected.

There's no excuse; but as explanation, I was ashamed. Not so much for using PEDs, as I already explained. I was ashamed because of how much of a mess it made for everyone. I was a "player's player," a good teammate, and what happened impacted my teammates past and present.

I was still enslaved to my ego, my reputation as a "man's man" at this point too. I was an island, a man who could handle anything. I didn't do vulnerability, and suddenly it was being forced upon me. And it acted as a paralytic. So, I didn't reach out to many people, and that's a great regret of mine. I have since reconnected, but it wasn't until many years later—after my darkest days.

THE END

A lot of players did what they felt they needed to do to perform their best. While we didn't talk about it, it's common knowledge. So, everyone in baseball knew I wasn't the only one who tried to extend his career, who did whatever he could to compete. But at the end of the day, I was the fall guy, the one who got caught, the face of the controversy. So, I took the brunt of the blame, and in those early days, the brunt of the angry backlash from the players, press, and fans. And to some extent, I still do to this day. Here's an excerpt from that ESPN piece done in 2007. I think it sums up the state of things pretty well:

> Since special agents from the IRS raided Grimsley's
> temporary home in Scottsdale, Ariz., early during the
> 2006 season when he was playing for the Diamond-
> backs and made him one of the initial suspects in
> baseball's burgeoning performance-enhancing drug
> scandal, the journeyman relief pitcher has lived, by
> most accounts, a little like a character tucked away
> in a federal witness protection program. Within
> days of the raid, he bolted from Arizona's clubhouse
> and retired to this quiet, sprawling suburb south of

Kansas City to hunker down with family and close friends and try to keep the outside world at bay.

He hasn't given interviews, and didn't for this story. His family is reluctant to shed much light on his season out of the game, believing he has been mistreated by the media. His minister, whose church Grimsley supported with a $140,000 donation from the money gained in a contract settlement with the Diamondbacks, has refused to utter a peep about him without the approval of his benefactor. And his Phoenix-based criminal defense attorney, Edward Novak, remains quiet. . . .

"He is not interested in doing any interviews," says longtime agent Joe Bick.

And it was true. In fact, I gave my whole salary to charity that year. I didn't play so I didn't deserve it. I went into hiding, only coming out for that day with the grand jury. I remember feeling a sense of closure and relief regarding the legal aspects of the whole thing, and in the days and weeks ahead, many of the speculations and untruths written in articles would be retracted. Of course, when it comes to retractions, they never get the same attention as the salacious lies, and that stuff is always out there. The salacious stuff is what sells, and there is always someone looking to make a buck.

Sometime after the grand jury, outside a New York bar with Dana, I was ambushed by TMZ—a little fella with a little camera and a light that shined on us. They had published a list that ranked the top cheaters in baseball from one to ten. I guess I was ranked number three.

And the guy asked, "Hey, how's it feel to be number three on the list?" as he danced around, expecting retaliation.

"Number three? That's bullshit, who was number one?" I responded.

It was the perfect approach to a TMZ article, but not for life. For years, I didn't let anyone in. And many wondered how I was able to laugh at myself. But what they didn't know was underneath, I was seething. Of course, I couldn't let anybody see my hurt or anger. That would be weakness, and I couldn't show any emotion or vulnerability. I put the whole thing into another box and put it away. It was just one more thing not to deal with.

In many ways, the way my career ended led to the darkest years, and ultimately darkest days, of my life. We'll talk more about that in the next chapter. That said, today, I have discovered grace. When I look back now, I can acknowledge the pain and loss and how my last days in baseball changed the game.

As Jeremy Jones said, "They (the League) let it get out of hand. They wanted better athletes. They wanted guys to throw the ball harder, hit the ball harder to sell more tickets. And whether people are in trouble (now), Major League Baseball is at fault, in my opinion."[28]

And at the end of the day, part of my story in baseball is that I was at the center of the PED witch-hunts and league-wide cleanup of the sport. It's a part of my history, and today I own it. Today, I am for testing and keeping the game clean.

But there are no do-overs, there are just consequences and the transforming grace of God. And I have known the first in great measure and the second as a measureless revelation.

CHAPTER TEN

The Darkest Day

I AM A ROCK, AN ISLAND

Covelli Loyce, aka Coco Crisp, gave me one of the biggest compliments of my career. He was asked one time in an interview which pitcher he most hated to face.

"That's easy," he responded, "Jason Grimsley."

"Why?" the interviewer asked in surprise. And he had good reason to be surprised. I wasn't a closer; I wasn't some big name.

Coco responded, "It's simple. You look out there and you realize that he doesn't care that you're standing in the batter's box. He doesn't care what you've done, who you've hit off; he's unshakable, unreadable, nothing seems to bother him."

It was one of the best compliments I ever got.

When I was on the mound, I didn't want the hitter to know one way or the other that I could be affected. When a hitter realized there was nothing he could say or do to get through to me—that nothing could touch me—it got in his head. I had built walls so I could perform. Like the famous Simon and Garfunkel song, "I [was] a Rock."

That served me well in baseball, but it nearly killed me in life. In baseball, especially as a pitcher, I needed to be able to set everything aside to perform. No situation that came up could bother me. But in life, *it is not good for a man to be alone.*[29] And by the time baseball ended, I was alone—a fortress none could penetrate.

HELL

As I've noted, I'm no theologian. I couldn't tell you much about heaven or hell after this life, but I know a good deal about it in the here and now. These days, I am learning about Jesus's prayer and how we pray that His will would be done "on earth as it is in heaven."[30] I'm learning to live confidently in God's love for me, but there was a time in my life when all I knew was hell.

Now, here is what I know to be true:

> God is love.
> He never leaves or forsakes us.
> Even if we make our bed in hell, He is with us.[31]

I've heard most preachers talk about hell as being the absence of God or the absence of love. I would argue, at least in this life, that hell is not the absence of God or love. Instead, it's the inability to recognize or receive His love, whether that's due to rejecting it, or sin, or loss, or trauma, or believing a lie, or abuse. At the end of the day, to me, hell is the inability to receive or experience love.

When I look back, God was walking with me even in my hell—especially in my hell. But I had no ability to sense God or love, from anyone. And that's hell. Hell isn't the absence of love; it's the inability to participate in love. It's the inability to open your heart to another person, to be vulnerable, to share in affection, generosity, or kindness toward yourself or others.

Hell is the inability to ask for help when you need it desperately.

Hell is the ache of loneliness while surrounded by your family and friends.

Hell is when you define yourself and others through your shame.

Hell is the desire to be transformed while convinced it's impossible to change.

Hell is the inability to forgive yourself and others.

Hell is when you are a rock or an island; it's when you have built a fortress around your heart that none can penetrate.

Hell is when you love your wife, kids, family, and friends with everything you are and yet continue to devastate them with your brokenness. Hell is when you believe they would be better off if you were dead.

AFTER BASEBALL

After baseball, I was completely lost. I didn't have a foundation. I was convinced Christ was no longer with me. I didn't feel like I deserved or was worthy of His love or anyone's love. I felt like a hypocrite everywhere I went. And looking back, I know now that it was the devil, banging on—lying to me about who I was and condemning me for it every step of the way.

I ended up in rehab in 2006. It was not a Christ-centered thing; I went there because if I didn't, Dana was pretty much done. I ended up in the psych ward. It didn't work. Partly because I was still not letting anyone in, but also because I knew my "higher power," and it was no fucking doorknob.

If that statement sems strong it's because I have strong feelings about rehab centers that aren't grounded in Christ. They worked a lot better before the government secularized them and turned God into a "higher power" which could be translated by anyone as anything, including a doorknob.

You have to understand, I wanted to be transformed, but I couldn't let anyone in to help me. As soon as I got out, I went right back to the old habits. The next years were a downward spiral. I have no idea what all I did in the darkest moments, in the throes of addiction—cocaine, drinking, meth, and cheating on Dana; anything I could do or get my hands on to change the way I felt, to numb the pain. I hid the worst of it from everyone; all but Dana. I hurt her so deeply over those years and the shame of how I lived became too much to bear.

Finally, in 2015, I came to a point where maybe I didn't want to exist anymore. Darkness was everywhere, an opaque nothingness. It encapsulated my soul. I could recognize light, and joy, and hope, and life. I could see it in my family, my friends; they seemed alive in every moment, content, and happy. But I couldn't enjoy anything; I felt nothing except pain and futility.

I had everything and yet there was nothing. And it was all my fault. There was no one else to blame. There was no way to right the wrongs, my wrongs. There was no way I could ever be forgiven. There was no way I could forgive myself. Hopelessness was my only companion. Even desperation was gone. I couldn't even access self-pity. My ego had exhausted itself, self-reviling and hoarse with rage.

I was alone. In a room full of friends and family, I was all alone. I had failed everyone and everything. I tried to fake it. I tried to drown it all out with vodka and cocaine—anything to mute the thoughts and feelings. I'd be numb for a brief time but never relieved, the pain would come crashing back in, more forceful than before.

I wanted to escape.

I wanted to be someone else.

I was jealous of everyone and everything.

Nothing helped.

Regret was my constant companion.

I was tired of the battle.

If this was living, I wanted no part of it.

I wanted it all to stop.

I surrendered to the inevitable.

"Everyone will be better off if I am no longer a disappointment or a distraction," I thought, over and over. It became the only thought that promised relief. I had given up on myself, my life, my family, everything. I was tired of living.

My cousin had a ranch, and there was a little bunkhouse on it. I purposely got in a fight with Dana so I could get away from everybody and ended up with an ounce of cocaine, about six bottles of vodka, and who knows how much beer. I decided this was going to be it. I spent three days in the depths of darkness trying to drink and drug myself to death, but it didn't work.

THE DARKEST DAY

In the bunkhouse, I agonized for the millionth time. "Why can't I stop. Why can't I control my behavior? Why do these voices keep tormenting me?" I didn't have an answer. And I had only one solution.

I wish I could tell you I can't remember what happened next. I wish I would have blacked out. I didn't. After three days of beer, vodka, and cocaine, I was still breathing. That's when I wrote my letters, my shameful goodbyes. Then I did the last of the cocaine, drank another glass of vodka, grabbed my pistol, and walked out into the woods. I found a place, sat down, cocked the gun, turned it, put the barrel to my left eye, and pulled the trigger.

My eye was open and looking down the barrel. I could see the rifling inside the barrel. I had wanted to see it coming.

But nothing happened.

I couldn't pull it again.

I remember the next hours as a fog. I was still in a dark place, but somehow, I was alive. Did something keep me alive? I got up and just started walking aimlessly through the woods. I felt like I was invisible. Animals took no notice of me. A copperhead literally slithered by my shoe and never seemed to notice me. A black buck walked within twenty yards, looked directly at me, and then kept walking.

For about six hours I wandered, until the sun started setting. I had nowhere to go. I don't remember being thirsty even though it was a hot day. Finally, I sat down against a pine tree. I just sat there, somehow alive and yet dead at the same moment.

I remember thinking, "Okay God, what now?"

By this time my family, friends, and the authorities were actively searching for me. A close friend of the family, Warren Despain, who was the constable for the county, found me. How he came upon that particular tree in the middle of the woods, I'll never know. God had to direct him. He asked for the gun. I obeyed and gave it to him.

I remember walking with Mr. Despain until we came across a group out looking for me. My cousin Terry, my best friend, was with them. He came running to me, grabbing me in his arms and weeping. He thanked God that I was alive, but I was numb.

The ride back to the lodge on the property was a blur. When we arrived, there were people everywhere. Dana, my children, my parents, my brother, my cousins, aunts, uncles, friends, and people I hadn't seen in years. Everyone was looking for me and everyone was overjoyed by the fact that I was still alive. What I had done did not have the effect I'd thought it would. I realized then that I actually mattered to people.

And in that moment, I was not the man's man, a man not to be messed with, the man nothing could touch. I was weak and vulnerable and broken and all of them could see it—and yet they loved me. I was still in trouble, still deeply broken, but there was no more hiding it.

That moment was the beginning of a long journey toward repentance, transformation, redemption, and reconciliation. But to tell that story, I first need to let some of those who loved me into wholeness share with you how what I did impacted them.

FROM THOSE I LOVE

As I wrote in chapter two, I believe family and friendship is the story God is telling. I think Jesus revealed the nature of the relationship between God and humanity in the context of family and friendship. Jesus called God "Dad."

This relational God is what I'm awakening to each day, specifically since my darkest day.

And that dark day is a part of my story, but not just my story. The brokenness in my life and what I did on that day greatly impacted everyone I love. I have since walked out healing and restoration, first between God and myself but also with my family and friends.

You see, every decision impacts the world around us, and my suicide attempt might as well have been like setting off a bomb in my relationships.

So, while I wanted to share my perspective, I didn't feel like it would capture the whole story without my family's perspective as well. That was a dark day for all of us. And a day in which I not only had to walk out forgiveness and healing for myself, but I also had to seek forgiveness and walk through healing with my family.

It's been a daily process of restored trust, where I am not only learning how to be vulnerable with myself and God, but with family and friends as well. So, with my friend and writer, Jason Clark, we interviewed some of my family about that day and put it together for this chapter.

Mom: We were eating at Roadhouse. It was my granddaughter's birthday. We'd gone down there to celebrate. Joe, Lynn, and Justin; Preslei, Chandler, the babies—I think Brylei was one year old, maybe a little over.

Joe got a phone call. It was my nephew, Jake, my sister's youngest son. I saw the color go out and Joe's face. I mean, it turned white. Joe hung up and didn't really want to say anything. He was in shock. Then he told us that Jason's truck was out at the ranch; that Dana had called Jason's uncle to check in on him because he had missed Rayne's volleyball game and that he'd found letters and Jason wasn't there.

Dana: The kids never really knew what he was up to or how broken he was until that night—even in 2006 when he first went to rehab. They didn't know back then that he was drinking or doing drugs. All they knew was that he was sick and needed to get help. They also didn't know he had cheated on me back then and I'd kicked him out.

I remember shortly after he left, I got a call from one of his friends saying he wasn't doing well and needed help. "Go help him, then," I said angrily. I was done. His friend took him to a psychiatric ward.

That evening, I came home thinking I was a single mom of three children, and while shutting the hatch to my car, I sensed God's voice: "He's your husband, and you need to take care of him." That's not a "thus saith the Lord" instruction for anyone reading this, because we all have to hear God for ourselves. But it's my story and an important part of it. It wasn't easy, but looking back, I know it was good.

So, I visited him in the psych ward. It was the worst thing I'd ever seen in my life. I felt so bad for him. I still loved him and knew he didn't belong there. With help, we got him into rehabilitation. Then, he moved back home and was clean for a little while. Thankfully, the kids didn't know anything about it. He was a good dad. Even when everything was falling apart, he went to all their sporting events and prayed with them every night.

But from 2006 through 2015, everything started falling apart between us. It started with my brother's death by suicide. They were close and that hit him hard. Then there was the airplane that crashed into our home, killing five people on board. That was in Kansas City and would have killed Rayne and me if we'd been in the wrong room. Then there was the death of his grandmother. And finally, losing baseball the way he did. In those ten years, everything between us was all about survival. And no one really knew the whole of it but us.

Somewhere along the way, he started drinking and doing drugs and cheating on me again. He still prayed with the kids at night, still showed up to sports events, still participated in family events, but I knew he wasn't well. And by 2015 God's words to me—"He's your husband and you need to take care of him"—felt like an empty, foolish promise. Our marriage was pretty much over.

In August, I'd had enough and told him he needed to move out. From there, I think he spiraled. While I could only guess at the amount of cheating, drugs, and drink he participated in, I knew he'd ended up at his cousin's bunk house out at the ranch. But it was out of character for him to not show up at Rayne's volleyball game.

Rayne: I was fifteen or sixteen at the time and in high school. They had been fighting really bad, but I didn't really know what it was about. So, my dad left to go to the ranch for a few days. I hadn't really talked to him. I was kind of upset that he just left. But I had a volleyball game, and on the bus ride there with all my teammates, I got a call from him.

"Hey, I just wanted to call and tell you I love you. You'll be great," he said.

"Are you coming to my game?" I asked. He paused and didn't answer. "Dad, are you gonna be there?" I asked again. "Yeah, I'll be there. I love you."

"Okay," I responded, but I did not say "I love you." I was so hurt that he was gone in the first place, I just hung up.

We played our match. Mom was there. But the whole time, I was looking for my dad, and he never showed up. He'd never done that to me. He'd never told me he was going to be somewhere and then not shown up for me—especially for sports events. But he never came.

I got in the car with my mom and asked, "Where's Dad?"

"I don't know," my mom answered. "We had a good conversation over the phone earlier. But he's not answering. He was supposed to be here; I don't understand. I haven't heard from him."

We picked up pizza and went home.

Dana: So, I called Terry's dad, Uncle Mack, because he's always on the ranch. I asked if he'd seen Jason and told him Jason was not answering his phone.

"Well, I didn't see him, but his truck was there," he responded. "I'll go check on him."

He didn't call me back. Apparently, he went into the bunkhouse, saw all Jason's letters, and called his son Terry because Terry and Jason are really close.

Rayne: I remember eating pizza while Mom made phone calls and hearing information like, "I saw his truck there." Then Mom started talking again about how she didn't understand and how he'd never done this before. I was so angry. I threw down my food and yelled, "You're the reason he left!" Then I ran to my room.

Dana: Terry is who ended up calling me. He said, "You need to get out here. We can't find him and something's wrong."

Mom: I remember getting up. The restaurant was so crowded, and I didn't want to scream right there at the table. Preslei had Brylei in the car seat carrier and the look on everybody faces was just—I don't know how to describe it. But when I got into the car, I just screamed. I mean, I thought he was gone.

John: I got a call from him that morning. I don't know who else he called, but I got a call from him that day, and I didn't answer. Later, I heard the voicemail something didn't feel right. And for a long time after, I wondered, "What if I'd just answered the phone?"

Dana: Our oldest son, Hunter, and our daughter and youngest, Rayne, were home when I got the call. John, our middle son, was at school for baseball in Houston.

Rayne: I was sitting in my room when I heard this scream, and I knew instantly something was very, very wrong. I ran into the kitchen, and Mom was talking to Terry. She was saying, "What do you mean you can't find him?"

I was getting bits of information, like his gun was missing. Mom was crying and yelling, and I dropped to my knees and started dry-heaving and screaming and crying. I was so angry. I thought my dad was gone and I was screaming at God, "You took him!"

Hunter: We were at the house. I had one of my close buddies over at the time. We were hanging out, and I heard my mom. It was terrible. She kept saying "No, no," over and over.

I ran into the kitchen, and she said, "They can't find your dad, and he left notes to each one of us. We gotta go."

She was borderline hysterical, and I remember holding her up at one point, saying, "Hey, it's okay. We'll get in the car. Let's go."

I remember it rained. I drove Mom and Rayne going 100 miles an hour down the highway with the hazards on, trying to get there. And I just remember thinking, "There's no way he'd do it. There's no way."

Rayne: Hunter had his hazards on, and he was driving really fast. And my mom was calling every single person she knew and asking them to pray. "Please pray, we can't find Jason. We don't know where he is."

John: Dad went through the same thing with my mom's brother. He actually received a call from Uncle Derek just before he committed suicide and wasn't able to answer. And for years, he wrestled with the same thoughts that I had: "What if I'd answered my phone? Maybe I could have done something." Yeah, so that was tough; that was really hard.

Hunter: One of my dad's least favorite words in the English dictionary is "can't." "Can't is for losers, quitters," he'd say. In my mind, for him to kill himself was the ultimate quit. I just couldn't imagine him doing it. Plus, my dad wasn't a loser.

John: Those hours when we didn't know where he was and didn't think he was alive were probably the worst in my life.

Dana: And so, Hunter drove us, and Rayne and I were sitting in the back. We were all crying. We didn't know what was going on, and I was feeling responsible—because, you know, I threw him out.

And we were having a hard time getting there because it was out in the woods at night. It's hard to find during the day, but trying to find it at night—well, we couldn't get there, and we were on the phone with Terry and honking the horn. "Can you hear us honk the horn? I feel like we're close, but can you hear us honking the horn?"

Rayne: I couldn't speak. I was in shock and thought for sure he was gone. I remember thinking, "I lost my best friend," because that was my dad. He was and still is my best friend, my protector. Thoughts flooded in: "I won't have anyone to walk me down the aisle. I'm not gonna have a dad anymore."

Mom: We finally found the ranch, and there were so many people already there—Jerry Mack, Warren Despain. As we drove up, while I was still in the truck, my sister called. She was crying but she said, "Judy, they found him. He's okay. He's alive."

Dana: Right when we pulled up, Terry called: "They found him, he's alive."

Hunter: And I felt huge relief.

Rayne: You would think that I would have felt relief, but I think I was in shock. I felt confusion. I'd believed my best friend had just passed away, that my dad was gone, and then all of a sudden, they found him.

Hunter: There were cops and a bunch of cars; my grandparents were out there, my uncle, lots of family; his friends from Cleveland—all out there.

Rayne: There were so many people. People I'd never seen before, too. As soon as we got out of the car, they were hugging me.

Mom: Jerry Mack said that when they were looking for him, they went to a deer stand. They noticed one of the rungs going up the ladder was muddy. Jerry Mack said, "I'm not going up there." And Warren Despain said, "I'll go." They thought they might find Jason up there.

Dad: Warren, he lives right down the road. He found Jason. Jason handed him the gun. To this day, every time I see him, he asks about Jason and how everything is going.

Dana: He didn't look like himself at all. He was so skinny.

Rayne: He was in the shop. My brothers and I sat down, and I looked at him. He was so skinny, almost unrecognizable. He didn't even look up. He was just staring at the ground.

I felt like I couldn't speak—like there was nothing I could say. But I wanted to say something about the Lord so badly. Finally, I got the words out, "Dad, God's gonna take care of you." He looked at me then and said, "Rayne, God wants nothing to do with me." And I was silent after that. I had no words.

Hunter: I remember seeing him as frail—just skin and bones, pale, drained completely. I'd never seen him like that. I knew him as the guy who worked out two times a day—a massive man. Suddenly, he was frail—he looked like I could beat him in a fight. He was vulnerable.

I remember a conversation we had shortly after when he said, "I couldn't do it. Does that make me a pussy?"

"No, you're a pussy for even thinking about doing that," I responded.

John: After we found him, there was a lot of relief, followed by anger. A whole lot of anger. I was furious with him.

Dad: It didn't hurt me near as bad as it made me madder than hell. That he would do that—it made me angry!

Mom: It was horrible!

John: For years, there was a lot of animosity toward him. We didn't have an honest conversation until I forgave him. I have wrestled with some of the same addictions as my dad, and I realized years ago at rehab I needed to forgive him. So, when Mom and Dad came to visit, I pulled him aside and said, "I never forgave you and I need to do that." And I did. It was tough, but I was able to realize how much my unforgiveness affected me and my relationships with others.

Hunter: After the suicide attempt, I knew he needed help, but I also realized it was going to be tough for the rest of the family—my mom, my brother, my sister. I knew, obviously, it was tough for him; I knew he felt he'd let us down. But I felt a sense of responsibility to make sure Mom, my sister, and my brother were okay.

Rayne: I didn't realize I hadn't forgiven my dad until I started to have bad anxiety. I never wanted to tell him how what he did hurt me because I was afraid it would make him fall back in that place and I'd lose him again. But once I did, he didn't respond the way I was afraid he might.

"I'm so sorry. I'm so sorry," he said. He told me he loved me and that he understood. He wasn't defensive, and he didn't take the position of a victim. He owned up to it completely, and he held me as I cried.

John: After that, he's become my friend. I always wanted to be my dad. He was and is and always will be my hero—that's not going to ever change. So, I always wanted to be my dad. And I've had to wrestle through some of the same things. But we're able to be really open with each other, and my dad is my best friend. He has been for a long time. I see God through him. He's modeled the way forward for me as I have had to wrestle through some of the same stuff.

Rayne: I think over time when Dad came home, I began to see this miraculous change within him. I began to see him and my mom working on their relationship.

First and foremost, I saw my mom's unconditional love; that was so restorative and so needed in their relationship and in our family. My mom held us together. I don't know how she did it. I've never come across a stronger woman. She believed in my dad, and she understood what it was to honestly live out a redeeming love.

God used my mom to heal my dad. Just through her sticking by and not leaving when everyone else told her to leave him. And I was a witness to everyone else telling her to give up on their relationship.

I think the Lord, over time, has healed them both so much. I started seeing them on their knees every morning, both of them in prayer, both of them in the Word, and I saw the community coming together and pouring into their lives. I saw my dad going to Bible study and men's groups. And slowly I began to see so much healing within him.

Hunter: For me, it was healing just seeing him go from trying to do everything on his own to cutting through everything and opening up to God. Seeing him go from frail to building his strength. And just him talking about his story and how God brought him back. There's a passion that he has that I haven't really seen since his baseball days.

John: In reality, a lot of the way I see God is through him—that kind of redemption we saw through him. The turnaround because he was at a very dark place. We didn't necessarily see everything that was going on. But years later, we definitely can see a change—a physical and mental, just an overall change inside of him that makes him a different person. And there's nothing in this world that can bring about that kind of change except the love of God.

Hunter: I love that Dad is writing this book, too; he has a really cool story. His walk with God and the stories he has about playing baseball. Like I said, to me, he is the coolest man on the face of the earth, without a doubt.

Rayne: You know, my dad isn't perfect. My mom's not perfect. I'm not perfect. Our family is not perfect. But I see the Lord's work and protection all throughout our lives. And I see the Lord transforming my heart. And my dad's heart, my mom's, my brothers'—and that's just our story.

You know, change doesn't happen all at once. It takes time to heal. And it takes time to really create a masterpiece, and that's what the Lord has done. And He's not finished yet. And thank goodness that He's not, you know. But one day, we will be completely restored and in a perfect relationship with Him. That's the day that I look forward to. And I'm thankful He has shown me redemptive love—and that you don't give up on those that you love—through my parents.

SALVATION

For the next year, I struggled with what I'd done. The shame and condemnation I felt for what I put my family through, what I put Dana through, weighed heavy on me. Then one day, on my face, I had a meeting with God that changed everything. It was subtle, but it was true. It was simple but deeply profound.

I cried out to God through tears, "I'm yours. I'm done fighting. I surrender."

And I meant it.

There was no explosion, no immediate miracle or sense of change, but I can now tell you exactly what happened. I discovered the foot of the cross that day. It's that place where you lay down your life fully— where you not only repent of your sins, but where you also admit your needs. It's where you leave everything, where you trust fully, where you are vulnerable.

I'd already asked Jesus into my heart. I'd already asked him to forgive me of my sins. But I have come to learn that's not what saves you from a life of misery. What saves you is when you let Him in and allow Him access to everything—every dark corner, full honesty, full stop.

For all those theologians, I'm not talking about some after-life salvation, I'm talking about that Greek word Jesus loved to use to describe salvation: *Sozo*. It means "to save, keep safe and sound, to rescue from danger or destruction."[32]

But it is not only meant to apply to the afterlife, it's also about wholeness and life now. It is both. You see, it also means "to save a suffering one . . . to make well, heal, restore to health."[33] This is not just physical health, but emotion, spiritual, relational health. Salvation is about wholeness being available in every aspect of our lives. Jesus died so we could be made whole.

What saved me from the failures and downfalls of my past wasn't my prayer, it was when I become vulnerable, when there was nothing hidden. That is the birthplace of trust. A place where love can be felt and known, where we can discover the kindness of God that leads to the changing of the way we think. It is where we begin to awaken to our oneness with God and discover that "in Him we live and move and have our being."[34]

Essentially, that day when I prayed, I decided to trust that God was good and gave Him the most important thing to me: my vulnerability. And that was the day I began to awaken to the joy of my salvation.

Now, once again, I'm no theologian, but I am writing about salvation as both a moment and a journey. Some might use the words "justification" (that instant when we are saved from our sins by God's grace through the redeeming love of Christ) and "sanctification" (that life-long journey of walking with Jesus and being transformed more and more into the image of Christ). The word "awakening" is a good one because it recognizes how daily surrendering our lives to the love of God impacts us over the course of time. And that is what began to happen. My salvation took place in a moment but is evidenced through daily choosing vulnerability.

After that prayer time, I actually got up on stage at our church. I stood in front of the whole body and said, "I'm struggling. I don't know what I'm doing. I don't know where I'm going. I just know that I need God, I need help."

I need help.

I am vulnerable.

Those were words I'd never owned. Words I couldn't say before that moment at the cross with a good and trustworthy God.

In the past I'd recognized failure, admitted to screwing up. I had confessed I had problems and that I was a sinner, but all those confessions were for mercy and forgiveness. And mercy and forgiveness were something I hoped to earn through confession. But none of my confessions were made in my weakness, none were admissions to my fears, and none were made from vulnerability. They were made in service to my ego.

In Matthew 16:24, Jesus says, "'If anyone would come after me, let him deny himself and take up his cross and follow me'" (ESV). For me, what Jesus was saying was, "Give me your ego and all that comes with it—sin, pain, sorrow, brokenness and shame; then give me your trust, your vulnerability, your friendship."

Until that prayer at the foot of the cross, my "Christian faith" had simply been another expression of my reputation as a man's man, a guy to be taken seriously, not to be messed with. A man who could never show weakness.

But that day at the cross, I began a journey into freedom.

And that day in front of the church was also huge, because I wasn't taking the journey alone. You see, when you admit you need help, you quickly become open to receiving it. Let me put it another way: you can't receive what you won't admit you need.

After that I got connected with a man named Michael Smalley. He showed me that a man's man can be a Christian—there was no stereotype for being a Christian. A Christian is about being wholly who God made you to be. Michael became a big influence and a great mentor. He helped me to continue down the road of living out my salvation, to pursue a "nothing hidden" life between God and me. And I continued to be set free and discover wholeness.

NOTHING HIDDEN

One day my AA sponsor was taking me through the fourth and fifth steps:

> 4. Make a searching and fearless moral inventory of ourselves.
> 5. Admit to God, to ourselves, and to another human being the exact nature of our wrongs.

After going through the steps with him, he said, "You left something off. You might not realize it now but call me when you do. It might be when you're heading home or tomorrow. But you're gonna want to tell me something that you didn't tell me now."

I got in my truck and said, "Shit!"

"Shit, shit, shit," I kept saying as I started driving, arguing with myself, not wanting to tell him.

Then I called him on the phone, "You're right."

"I'm still here, come on back," he responded.

I was scared but not like I had been in the past. I wanted freedom so much, and I had already become vulnerable with God. So, I told him about my childhood, about the abuse and the shame. As he listened, I felt this weight lift. A thousand tons suddenly gone. He prayed over me, let me know God had always been with me, that He loved me and was always with me. And I knew he was right. Then he encouraged me to share with a counselor and with Dana.

I did.

I was forty-eight years old when I told Dana what happened to me as a kid. This was the beginning of a deeper work in our marriage. So many of our broken places were connected to that hidden event. Shame and condemnation had been allowed to grow for so long, and suddenly I was set free from it.

Over time, I could see these evil twins' impact on so much of my life and our marriage. So much of Dana's feelings of disconnection and insecurity over the years had been caused by that brokenness in me. As we talked together, she could understand why I was distant and would be willing to kill myself—why I would do that to her and the kids. Grace and mercy began to flow in our marriage as we sought further counseling.

I am not dismissing what I did. There's no excuse for the pain I caused, and it was real. But for the first time we had a sure hope for healing.

It has taken years and will continue to be a journey of growing in trust and reconciliation in our love for each other. There are no quick solutions to the hurt caused; there's no fast-track. Trust takes time, and I am learning that wholeness is discovered when I live vulnerably with her as well.

Nothing hidden.

And that's scary and beautiful and where life is discovered.

There have still been moments when hell feels just around the corner—when the Enemy attempts to seduce me by stroking my ego with the familiar lies of power and control. But daily I am learning how to resist the devil and instead choose grace unto salvation.

And I have experienced such grace. You see, I didn't think my relationship with my wife and my kids was repairable. But today I am a rich man—rich in the love of my family and friends.

NOT WITHOUT YOU

Michael Smalley helped a lot with Dana and my relationship.

But above all, it was Dana who saved our marriage; she didn't abandon ship. And it is a testament to her faith, her conviction, and her love for me and her family that she was willing to—for better or worse, rich or poor, sickness and health—pursue restoration.

I remember a seminal moment shortly after the suicide attempt between Dana and me. I was in rehab, and everything was pretty shaky between us. I was still struggling with shame, and our marriage was a huge question mark. She came to me and said, "This does not work without you."

God, those words were powerful.

To this day I'm blown away by them.

The invitation to reconciliation was God-like. I saw her love for the Lord and for me. For her to be able to say that after what I put her and my family through—that was a moment where things really started to turn around, when I began to get better. That was only one of many God moments. There has been so much healing from the love she showed me, even when she didn't like me!

And over the years, I began to experience healing through the love my kids showed me, the love I've felt from my family. The way my mom, my dad, my brother, my cousin, and my friends rallied around me. It's been humbling and transforming.

But Dana is the best way for me to get my bearings. She is a trustworthy friend, my best friend, and I owe her my life. She's definitely the rock who loves the Rock. That's not to say our marriage is perfect.

There are still challenges and blowups as we learn how to be patient with each other, but Dana knows I'm not going anywhere. I know she's not going anywhere. And our kids see that. And that's beautiful. A miracle.

You see, I am learning I am not here to do something for God, I am here to know and be known by God.

To be known by God is the salvation Jesus died and rose again to give us access to. In John 17, Jesus prayed that we would know oneness with Father God like He knew oneness. Jesus prayed that we would not just know how to serve God but that we could become friends with God. Jesus wanted us to have a relationship, and relationship is about vulnerability. A relationship is only as deep as how well we know one another. To know and be known by God is the joy of our salvation.

The first time I was saved, I thought there was something I had to do to change the world for God. I was on fire, but I thought there was something I had to do to deserve my salvation. I thought, "I got it, now I gotta go earn it." It's silly but it's what I thought and what so many think.

Now I am not earning anything, I am just receiving. And that's the gospel. Again, I'm no theologian. But the gospel, or the good news, to me, is that I am loved. It's not about earning or deserving; it's about believing and receiving.

But here's the crazy thing: When you live that way, you can't help but give love away.

Yankees chaplain George McGovern invited me to Ohio a few years ago and I had a chance to share my story. And the impact humbled me. And that's when I started to pray about telling my story.

CHAPTER ELEVEN

A Testimony

THE OTHER TEAM

There's a scene in the Brad Pitt baseball movie *Moneyball* where Chris Pratt, who plays Oakland Athletics first baseman Scott Hatteberg, hits a homerun that forever changes the course of how analytics are viewed in baseball.

It's the scene in the movie where everything hangs in the balance, where careers will be made or lost, where risk pays off. Indeed, the homerun proves that the Oakland A's GM, assistant GM, and manager (played by Brad Pitt, Jonah Hill, and Philip Seymore Hoffman, respectively) are the real deal—forward-thinking, successful baseball guys. It's that part of the movie where the team comes together and wins. You know, the part of the movie you've been waiting for.

Well, for there to be a homerun hitter, there has to be a pitcher who threw him the ball. The movie uses actual footage for this scene, and if you watch closely, you might notice that pitcher is me. And if you pause it at the right moment, you'll see my face as I realize Scott just hit a dinger off me. I'm pissed. And if you read lips, my reaction is R-rated.

I loved competing. I loved being on a team and against the others. The clear objective and combative nature of it—loved winning and hated losing. And I was serious about games and intensely focused before and during them. So, if you weren't on my team, I didn't make time for you.

Sandy Alomar, Jr.—a catcher for the Indians who I played with for three years, and a very good friend—tried to catch up with me before a game one time. Problem was, Sandy and I were no longer on the same team. He had a different uniform than me, which meant I wasn't interested in talking. There was no fraternizing before a game.

"I'll talk to you after the game," I kept saying. But he ignored me and kept talking; he interrupted my pre-game preparation for ten minutes! Finally, we hugged and joined our respective benches.

When Sandy got to bat in the game, on my first pitch, I hit him right in the middle of his back. He threw his bat and looked at me confused and pissed. I yelled, "I told you, I didn't want to talk to you before a game."

Anybody who was wearing another uniform was trying to take something from me. That was my mindset. And I didn't care if it was my best friend, like Jeff Grotewold.

In 1992, the year Dana and I got married, we went to Venezuela so I could play in their baseball league. It's called winter ball, and a lot of players would go down in the MLB offseason and play for a Venezuelan team. It was a lot of fun, especially with the wives.

That year, I played in their World Series for the Magallanes while Jeff played for the opposing Zulia team. Jeff was newly married as well, and Dana met his wife, Teresa, for the first time at that game. They sat together.

The game started, and right away I struck the first two guys out. Then up came Jeff. He knew if I got ahead of him with a strike, he was as good as out. I threw him a four-seam fastball; he guessed right and hit it out of the ballpark. I wasn't happy, especially when he started laughing on his way to first base. I met him at third and I spat on him.

"Did you spit on me?" he asked incredulously.

"Yep, and when you get to bat again, I'm gonna hit you right in the middle of back."

Jeff's my best friend, but I made good on my word and drilled him right in the middle of his back next time he was at bat. When the game was over, we met up, and as we were walking out of the stadium, Dana and Teresa joined us.

"Did you spit on him?" Dana asked.

"Yeah," I said matter-of-factly.

He looked at her and said, "I shouldn't have laughed."

She looked at me and asked, "Did you hit him on purpose?"

"Yeah," I responded as though it were obvious.

She looked at him, and he said again, "I shouldn't have laughed."

In case you're wondering, we are all really good friends to this day; Jeff's Hunter's godfather.

But Jeff gets it. He understands how I'm wired and my combative nature within the game. Mutual respect is important to show toward the other team, but in the game, those players are the enemy, and I wouldn't make time for them.

I tend to look at most things in life that way. I tend to view my journey in the context of teams—what I am for and what I am against. I'm not talking about how I see people; we are all in the family, all God's kids, all on the same team—even the prodigals and older brothers. I'm talking about the game of life. In this game, there is an Enemy. And he is a liar, and I won't make time for his lies.

The devil isn't powerful; all he has is the lie. And it's one lie, but he presents it in a plethora of ways. It can sound like, "You're shameful, not enough, alone, unloved; you can't change; you should give up; God doesn't love you; there is no redemption for you."

The lie is the same one the devil used in the garden of Eden when the snake told Eve, "'God knows that when you eat from it your eyes will be opened, and you will be like God.'"[35] That lie suggested God was withholding a part of Himself from her, that He wasn't trustworthy and good. And that lie suggested she wasn't enough just as God had created her, that she was somehow lacking.

The fact is, God made Adam and Eve in His image; they were already like God, had everything they needed, and were whole. But that's what the Enemy attacks: he always lies first about God's good and perfect love for us, and then about our value, our worth.

He does this for a reason. He wants us to define our identity and value by our behavior. Why? Because *we have all sinned and fallen short* and we know it.[36] And he can use that to condemn and shame us; to make us feel worthless. But we can't define our identity or value based on our behavior. We must know who we are and determine our value based on God's love.

Our identity must rest in the blood of Jesus and in the fact that neither death nor life can separate us from His love.

We are in the game of life, and we can't make time for the lies of the devil. If we buy into his lies, it's likely we will find ourselves with a baseball in our back. Not from God—rather, it's simply the consequence of chasing our ego.

You see, in the game of life, winning isn't about "doing better"— that way only leads to shame and condemnation. Winning is about rejecting the liar and his lies; it's about submitting our hearts to the kindness of God. It's about surrender and trust and saying yes to the reconciling love of God revealed through Jesus on the cross.

LET'S GO SLOW

As I intimated at the end of the previous chapter, a few years ago I reconnected in a significant way with Yankees chaplain George

McGovern. He was instrumental in my spiritual growth after my attempted suicide. He helped me begin to discover what it meant to reject the lie of distance and shame and to live confidently in God's "always good" love. He helped me discover that the joy of my salvation is in learning how to love others as Christ did.

I would like to suggest that the more you discover God's forgiveness and reconciling love, the more access you will have to who you truly are; and who you truly are is a person who loves well.

There's a verse in Scripture that we use to rightly define why we are on the planet. It comes from the lips of Jesus Himself: "'Love the Lord your God with all your heart and with all your soul and with all your strength and with all your mind' and, 'Love your neighbor as yourself.'"[37]

But you can't give away what you don't have. That's why I keep bringing you back to 1 John 4:19: "We love because He first loved us." You can't really engage in loving folks until you know the relentless, never-leaving love of God. But here's what I am learning: The extent to which you are sure of God's love for you is linked to the extent to which you can give it away. And that's a journey.

As I mentioned, the first time I got saved is when I said the sinner's prayer—it was like a bang, an explosion. The younger son came home to be embraced by his father! But then I became the older brother and over time it nearly killed me.

The second time I got saved, it was a slow burn, a humble flame, a daily walking out of my salvation. It was almost like God said, "I'm gonna show him a little bit of my love, then I'm gonna put a little more heat on the fire. But this journey isn't about going 100 miles an hour, and it's not about what you can do for me. It's about your discovery of the fullness of what I have already done for you, and for all humanity." It's like God wants me to simply grow sure in His love. Surer today than I was yesterday.

"Let's go slow," God has said to me. And it's a novel idea. As you know, I like to go fast. As the famous Ricky Bobby says, "If you ain't first, you're last." But some things are missed when you travel at excessive speeds, and God wants me to experience the journey differently. It's why I waited so long to write this book. Well, that, and I needed a little encouragement.

MR. ADAMS

Duwane Adams is a world-renowned Glasser; binoculars on a tripod is his innovation. If you are not familiar with the world of hunting, a Glasser is someone who's good at stalking and spotting game in the wild. Adams gives seminars and has a school that hunters the world over travel to so they can learn how to find animals. He owns a guide service. He is elite at his craft. He is also a good man and a Christian and has become a mentor to me over the last five years or so. He is one of the most encouraging voices in my life and was one of the first people to encourage me to write this book.

I met him a year or so after my darkest day. Here's what he had to say about when we first met.

> I met Jason when he came to hunt with me. He went out with one of my guides for three days, then I went out with him on the fourth.
>
> I always ask my clients what they do for a living. I take out a lot of movie stars and professional athletes. Most of them have a real arrogance about them, and I'm telling you the truth. I mean, you can hardly stand it.

I was glassing with Jason and asked, "Well, son, what do you do for a living?" I'm 67 years old, so I'm quite a bit older than Jason.

"Well Mr. Adams"—he always calls me Mr. Adams— "I played a little baseball."

I asked, "What kind of baseball, Jason?"

He said, "I played seventeen years in the big leagues."

Most people who have that kind of success can't wait to tell you and they cram it down your throat till it's almost embarrassing. I mean, you get sick listening to the stories, you know. That was not the case with Jason.

I said, "Jason, that's something to be very proud of."

He said, "I am proud of it, Mr. Adams, but it's not something to brag about. People don't need to hear it."

That statement was an insight to his character. I spent a few days hunting with him. He told me the story about how he tried to commit suicide and how he met Jesus. It was humble and powerful, and by the end of it I asked, "Jason, next January, when you come back, if I set it up in our church, would you give your testimony?"

"I'd be more than glad to, Mr. Adams," he said.

I have been doing what I do a long time and I have quite a following on Facebook and Instagram. I put out there that Jason was going to be sharing his story and they came from high and low—literally 150 miles to listen to him. I'm telling you, it was packed.

And Jason spoke from the heart. He touched a lot of people's lives. I think the boy has a tremendous ability to talk to people and not give them a bunch of crap. He can tell them the truth about what God has done in his life, which is unbelievable.

But what was most incredible is Jason's interaction with the people after the service. One person stood out to me. There was a girl who came to the front after Jason spoke. She hung back until most folks had gone, then she came up to him and said, "I came to listen to you, sir. I was going to commit suicide yesterday."

I wouldn't have known what to say. I've never been involved in anything like that. But Jason stood there, with a lot of people waiting and wanting to talk to him, and he truly loved, connected with, and encouraged her. He was just there for her.

For a long time, I thought my identity was as a baseball player, that my value was discovered in my ability to throw a ball. I thought that was why I was here. And yeah, that's part of my story, but that ain't the whole story. I'm still in the process, still learning why I'm here. But that day at Mr. Adams's church helped me get an idea of it.

I'm here to help people who are going through things that are similar to what I went through. I am here to help people get set free from the lies of the devil and discover the always-good love of their Savior and Father.

I'm here to let you know that regardless of where you are and regardless of how alone you feel—you're not alone. God created every living being in this universe. He knows you by name, He knew you before you were born, He knows you now, He loves you more than you can imagine, and you're not alone.

I spoke in two services at Mr. Adams's church. Before I got up the first time, the pastor asked, "Would you like to come down front after you speak and pray with anyone who comes up?"

"Yes."

So, I told my story, and you coulda heard a pin drop. I think everyone expected to get Jason Grimsley the pro ballplayer. Jason Grimsley, the man's man who could tell you all about the successes he'd experienced in all his years in baseball. And yeah, I shared some baseball stories. But then I shared the down and dirty, the story you've read in this book.

I told them about my fears and about the darkest day of my life. And then I told them about salvation, the fact that God loved me, redeemed me, and restored me. That He was setting me free, transforming and reconciling me. Then I told them that no matter where they were in their journey, God never, ever leaves.

After the first service a man came up and shared his story, about how he and his wife lost their son, and how he couldn't understand why. He said that while listening to me share vulnerably about the love of God, he felt like he could trust that God really loved his son and that God never left him. He thanked me and then gave me a cross he had made. He said, "I don't know who this is for, but I feel like I am supposed to give it to you." I thought it was incredible, but I didn't know who it was for, either. I thanked him, put it in my back pocket, and got ready for the second service.

I told my story again. And again, afterward I stepped off the stage to meet and pray with anyone who came up. After a while I noticed one lady, maybe in her 30s, hanging back. After I'd spoken to the last person, she approached me. She looked at me with tears in her eyes and said, "I don't know why I came to church today. I don't ever come to church, but I'm where you were on your darkest day—right now."

I talked with her, told her I knew how she felt, and shared how God loved her. Then I remembered the cross in my back pocket. I said, "There was a gentleman who came this morning and gave me this cross. He didn't know why he gave it to me, but I know now it was so I could give it to you." She cried as she received it.

I went on to tell her how God wasn't angry, how He was with her and would never leave her. And I acknowledged her pain with an empathy much like Jesus. I understood what she was going through, and she told me she felt that. She said she felt the hope of healing and wholeness because I was a walking testimony of what God could do.

As Christians, it's so important that we can be people who can let others know it's okay. You can mess up, but if you think you've messed up more than can be fixed, then somebody's lying to you. It's not true. There's nothing you can do that can't be undone.

TESTIMONY

Everybody has a story. Everybody is on a journey. And sharing it connects us to each other and to God. There have been many times since that day at Mr. Adams's church when I have had the opportunity to share my story and journey with churches, men's group homes (where guys are getting help to get back on their feet), and small groups. It is lifegiving to me and to those who are on similar journeys.

Sure, my story includes professional baseball and that's provided me a platform from which I can tell it. But my whole story isn't about baseball—it's about the never-leaving love of God. And yeah, I love telling baseball stories, but I really love telling the whole story of God's reconciling, transforming love that I continue to awaken to along the way.

The fame, fortune, and notoriety—all that stuff is not what this life is about. It's about the love of our Lord and Savior Jesus Christ, the love that He has for us revealed through the blood that was spilled. Life is about discovering that we are created in our God's image and that He loves us so much that He sent His son. It's about the salvation we discover though the cross.

I love to share my story, the one in which a self-centered, egotistical ballplayer got saved by a loving, kind, and reconciling God. And I love to tell my story because there is transformation available for others in it.

It's called a testimony and when we share it, we impact the testimony of others. For instance, check out how my testimony impacted my daughter Rayne's testimony. How my story is a part of her story, and how her story changed a life.

Here's the story in Rayne's own words:

> I went to Guatemala on a mission trip two years ago. We were providing water filters for families and sharing the gospel through that.
>
> We went to this one family's house one day and gave them a water filter. We showed them how to use it, all the while sharing the gospel with them. We were speaking through a translator, and I noticed an older man off to the side who wasn't engaging

much. I heard the Lord say to me, "You need to speak with him."

So, I went over and asked him about his life. While he communicated through the translator, I heard the Lord say, "Share about your dad."

Not many people in my group knew that story but I was like, "Okay God." So, I started telling the story about my dad, about his drug and alcohol abuse and how he eventually tried to take his own life.

Then I talked about the power of God's redemption, forgiveness, and love, and how much the Lord had changed my dad's life. How my dad had experienced God's saving grace and now had a daily relationship with the Lord. And then I talked about the transformation in my life because of what God had done in my dad; how it encouraged me in my own relationship with God.

The man started to cry. Then he shared a story about how his dad was also a drug addict and abused alcohol. Then he said, "I want that relationship you just described with God. I want that." My dad's testimony and my testimony met the man where he was, and his heart was touched. He gave his life to Christ in that very moment. All the way down in Guatemala, a man's life was changed because of my dad's story. That's the whole point to me.

Last year; a really close friend of mine was going through a nasty divorce. I was in a different country when I got the phone call from him. He was broken. "We're coming back tomorrow," I said. "As soon as we land, I'll head your way."

And I did. My eighteen-hour flight was followed by a several hours' drive up to his place. I was happy to go. I spent four or five days with the guy, and just loved on him.

Now, I have always been the kind of guy who would have a friend's back, the kind of guy who would drop everything for family or friend. Even those early days of baseball when I was building my reputation as a man not to be messed with, I had a generous heart for those who were hurting or vulnerable. I would often pull a $100 bill from my pocket for the homeless fella sleeping on the bench, and no one would know.

But in those days, I didn't have the testimony of my salvation; I wasn't daily awakening to a love that reconciles all of us. But now? Now I was able to visit my friend in one of his darkest days and love on him like Jesus loves on me.

Recently, Mr. Adams and I were grabbing lunch at his local diner when a couple of his friends walked up to the table. He introduced me to them as a former ballplayer, a pitcher who'd played twenty years, a Yankee with World Series championships. "Jason was one hell of a ballplayer," he said. "But he's an even better human being."

Even better. That is the greatest compliment and my prayer: that I could be a better man today than I was yesterday and a better man tomorrow than I am today. Not because of something I've done but because of something I'm discovering: God's love is perfect, and He saves and transforms our lives so we might be an expression of His love and salvation to another.

A MEMOIR IN PROGRESS

I can look to my future with hope and upon my past with thankfulness. And I can see God's redeeming, reconciling love at work on the good days and especially on the bad. I can see God was always with me.

He was with that passionate wild kid, He was there in my childhood, the glorious early days of baseball, and the wild living. He was there when I met the love of my life, there while we were making a family. God was there while I chased my baseball dreams and achieved them and in the friendships along the way. He was in the laughter, favor, food, and traveling. He loved me and He was always with me.

And God was with me as a child when I felt alone and afraid. He was there through broken bones and lost toes. He didn't leave me when I was abused or when I couldn't show weakness. He was there through the rejections and fears and struggles and pride and fights and ego and the self-medicating addictions. He was there when I broke my wife's heart and hurt my family.

And He is with me now as I share my story of His saving grace, transformation, and learning that redemption is marriage and family and friendship. God has never left me. He has always walked with me and has always known my fears and losses and joys. God has always loved me and has been reconciling my heart to his since I was a kid. And on the darkest days, where there was only one set of footprints, that is when He carried me.

If there is one thing I know, and one thing I am still learning, it's that God is love and He never leaves. I am convinced that "neither death nor life, neither angels nor demons, neither our fears for today nor our worries about tomorrow—not even the powers of hell can separate us from God's love."[38]

This is my memoir to date, my story, my testimony. God is good, He loves us, He never leaves us, and all things can be made new. And if there is one thing I hope for you, it's that you would also know this never-leaving, reconciling love of God on your journey.

Endnotes

1 Simon & Garfunkel, "Mrs. Robinson," track 3 on The Graduate, CBS, 1968, vinyl.

2 Matthew 27:46

3 Margaret Fishback Powers, *Footprints: The Story Behind the Poem* (Grand Rapids, MI: Zondervan, 1993), 9.

4 Psalm 22:14a, 15a, 16–20

5 Psalm 139:8 NKJV

6 See 1 John 4:19

7 Romans 8:38-39 NLT

8 Ed Parker, *Ed Parker's Encyclopedia of Kenpo* (Pasadena, CA: Delsby Publications, 1992).

9 Blockus, Gary, and The Morning Call. "Hoefling: The Man behind the Golden Arm." The Morning Call, October 1, 2021. https://www.mcall.com/news/mc-xpm-1984-07-05-2437605-story.html.

10 Gary Blockus, "Hoefling: The Man behind the Golden Arm," The Morning Call, July 5, 1984, https://www.mcall.com/news/mc-xpm-1984-07-05-2437605-story.html.

11 See Galatians 5:22-23

12 "Empathy," Cambridge Dictionary, accessed April 6, 2022, https://dictionary.cambridge.org/us/dictionary/english/empathy.

13 John 1:14

14 Ephesians 3:17-20

15 "Reconciliation," Cambridge Dictionary, accessed April 4, 2022, https://dictionary.cambridge.org/dictionary/english/reconciliation.

16 Robert Louis Stevenson, "La Fere of Cursed Memory" in *An Inland Voyage* (New York: P.F. Collier & Son, 1902), 99.

17 Buster Olney, "Yankee Ends Real Corker of a Mystery" (The New York Times, April 11, 1999), https://www.nytimes.com/1999/04/11/sports/yankee-ends-real-corker-of-a-mystery.html.

18 "Perfect Games in Baseball History." MLB.com. Accessed April 20, 2022. https://www.mlb.com/team/photos/perfect-games.

19 Luke 15:21-24 ESV

20 Luke 15:25-31

21 Mayo Clinic Staff, "Human Growth Hormone (HGH): Does It Slow Aging?," Mayo Clinic (Mayo Foundation for Medical Education and Research, November 13, 2021), https://www.mayoclinic.org/healthy-lifestyle/healthy-aging/in-depth/growth-hormone/art-20045735.

22 "Report: Wells May Have Edited Steroids Passage," ESPN (ESPN Internet Ventures, March 13, 2003), https://www.espn.com/mlb/news/2003/0303/1517374.html.

23 Joe Christensen, "Canseco Book: Players Injected Each Other," Baltimore Sun, February 7, 2005, https://www.baltimoresun.com/bal-sp.canseco07feb07-story.html.

24 "A-Rod Admits, Regrets Use of Peds," ESPN (ESPN Internet Ventures, February 9, 2009), https://www.espn.com/mlb/news/story?id=3894847.

25 "McGwire Apologizes to La Russa, Selig," ESPN (ESPN Internet Ventures, January 11, 2010), https://www.espn.com/mlb/news/story?id=4816607.

26 Mike Fish, "The Life and Times of Jason Grimsley since the Affidavit," ESPN (ESPN Internet Ventures, November 8, 2007), https://www.espn.com/mlb/news/story?id=3097689.

27 Ibid.

28 Ibid.

29 Genesis 2:18, author's paraphrase

30 Matthew 6:10

31 See Deuteronomy 31:6; Psalm 139:8; 1 John 4:8

32 "Sozo Meaning in Bible," biblestudytools.com (The NAS New Testament Greek Lexicon), accessed April 5, 2022, https://www.biblestudytools.com/lexicons/greek/nas/sozo.html.

33 "Strongs's #4982: Sozo," Bible Tools, accessed April 5, 2022, https://www.bibletools.org/index.cfm/fuseaction/Lexicon.show/ID/G4982/sozo.htm.

34 See Acts 17:28

35 Genesis 3:5

36 See Romans 3:23

37 Luke 10:27

38 Romans 8:38 NLT